BOO
OF THE
FUTURE

BOOK OF THE FUTURE

BBCi

Published on behalf of BBCi by BBC Worldwide Limited
80 Wood Lane, London W12 0TT

ISBN 0 563 48771 2

Commissioning Editor: Nicky Ross
Project Editor: Julie Tochel
Designer: Annette Peppis
Production Controller: Belinda Rapley

Set in Century, Eurostile, Helvetica, Impact, Linedraw, Nueva, Orbit,
Photina, Rockwell, Tarzana, Trajan, Space, Weisbaden Swing
Printed and bound in Great Britain by Martins the Printers Ltd, Berwick-upon-Tweed
Cover printed by Belmont Press, Northampton

Visit the Book of the Future website at
http://www.bbc.co.uk/future

contents

An ongoing conversation!

This book is the work of many people who submitted their work via the Book of the Future website in what was an experiment in developing a conversation on the future. Why should this book signal the end of the conversation? The website can be your gateway to getting involved and having your say.

Get talking to the various authors in this book (and the ones who didn't make it!) and leave your views on any of the articles by going to the website at <www.bbc.co.uk/future>. By adding either the author or the article number to the URL address you will be taken to either the article or author of your choice (e.g. <http://www.bbc.co.uk/future/A867549> or <http://www.bbc.co.uk/future/U42>).

Which do you like best? Have the public chosen the right ones? Why did the author write that about the future? Have your say and get involved in the ongoing book! Think of it as a never-ending literary lunch, without all the nice food.

Special thanks to our guest contributors who generously gave their time to write for the website and were brave enough to take on the competition (some more successfully than others!): Nick Baines, Ian Baker, Ian Banks, Ozwald Boateng, Clive Collins, Bernard Dixon, Zac Goldsmith, David Hobman, Barney Leith, David Levy, Paul Lewis, Tracey Logan, Trisha Macnair, Brian May, Michael Meacher, Ute Navidi, Tara Palmer-Tomkinson, Ian Pearson, Andrew Pinder, Jonathan Pugh, Ken Pyne, Noel Sharkey, Karol Sikora, Ralph Steadman, Edward Stourton, Thomas Sutcliffe, Robert Thompson and Irvine Welsh.

This book was Douglas Adams' idea. He knew that trying to predict the future is a mug's game, but he wrote that it is 'increasingly a game we all have to play. The world is changing so fast... we need to have some sort of idea of what the future is actually going to be like, because we are going to have to live there, probably next week.'

But there are so many predictions, it is hard to know who to believe. Even the most knowledgeable people frequently get it wrong. In the past, some have taken an overly pessimistic view of emerging technologies: Darryl F. Zanuck, head of Twentieth Century Fox, said of television's future, 'People will soon get tired of staring at a plywood box every night.' Others have been more bizarre: the Hoover Company stated in 1955, 'Nuclear powered vacuum cleaners will probably become a reality within ten years.'

Yet no one foresaw the impact of the microwave oven, Velcro, TV dinners, laser surgery, air bags and of course, the Internet. If experts can get predictions so wrong, is there any way of working out which are more accurate than others? Douglas Adams thought of a way: collect all the ideas from anyone, anywhere, about anything and store them on the Internet. In so doing, you would be able to capture a blueprint of the present reality that contained all the necessary information to hint at the future. By asking people to select the strongest ideas anonymously, you could reach a consensus on the most likely future. In scientific circles, this is called the Delphi technique.

Adams's company began gathering ideas from the public on the Hitchhiker's Guide to the Galaxy website. He and I also began to discuss how best to bring his ideas to life. After his untimely death in 2001, the BBC decided to keep the site going and rehoused it on BBCi. The Book of the Future sister site was created in October

2002 at www.bbc.co.uk/future, inviting people to submit specific predictions for the year 2020.

Nine months later, this book was born. Out of the thousands of entries, seventy-five of the best articles – submitted and rated via the website according to Delphi principles – are contained in the world's first democratically edited book. Inside, sixteen-year-old Lou from London stands shoulder to shoulder with the Rt Hon Michael Meacher, MP.

Projects like Book of the Future are about creating communities of interest, putting people in touch with one another and empowering them, not just to enjoy the BBC's ideas, but to publish their own. Increasingly people want to have their say, to debate and to discuss opinions with like-minded people. They want to contribute and shape the media they are enjoying. At BBCi – the part of the BBC that deals with the Internet, interactive TV and the techie

'I THINK THERE IS PROBABLY A WORLD MARKET FOR MAYBE FIVE COMPUTERS' THOMAS WATSON, CHAIR OF IBM, 1943

stuff – we passionately believe that this is the future.

This project was a collective effort involving many thousands of people online, but I would like to thank a few in particular. I am most obviously indebted to Douglas Adams whose brilliance enabled him to think up this project in the first place. I hope we have done it justice. A huge thank you goes also to Dave Gorman. Lastly, thanks and congratulations go to James Boardwell, Emily Angle, Jennifer Haslam-James, Catherine Wyler and Richard Williams at the BBC for bringing the site and the book to life.

Ashley Highfield,
Director of New Media and Technology, BBC.

Book of the Future

From: Dave Gorman
Sent: Tuesday 1 April 2003 11.59 am
To: Book of the Future
Subject: Comic Relief

Many people claim they can predict the future, but few have any credibility. For instance, there's an old man in my local who claims he can read your earwax. Mind you, he also claims he can guess a lady's weight just by tasting her nipple, so he's widely regarded as a crank.

Yes, the future, by its very nature, is a tricky blighter to pin down. But the brave souls who have contributed to this fine book have approached that uncertainty, not to mention the risk of ridicule, head on to come up with the most comprehensive vision of all of our futures ever assembled. And who knows if it might actually come true? The newspapers of today suggest we are on the brink of an in-utero, reality TV, micro-chipped technological dystopia and who knows, there might well come a time when some of us know what some of those words actually mean.

Why the BBC has given a platform for the rantings of such a psychologically disturbed populace in the name of charity, I'll never know. I suppose it has something to do with a notion of offering the terminally-deferential British an opportunity they'd never get by sending in their tapes to *You've Been Framed*: a chance to air their views on how to make the world a better place. Or at least to let everyone in the nation know the limits to which they'll go for a date in 2020.

I did offer a contribution myself, but this is a truly democratic publication and it seems that you, the public, have dismissed my article on the merits of its title alone. Quite why *The Future's*

Bright, The Future's Gorman should have been excluded is beyond me. After all, if wisely used, is the cloning of a Gorman army really so wrong?

Without question, some of the people who are as avid as I am in the pursuit of a brighter future are the hard-working folk at Comic Relief, to whom contributions from the project are being donated. If only all profits from books could be contributed to causes greater than, say, the Jeffrey Archer Legal Costs Fund. It may not be the most direct way of raising money – robbing banks, for example, is potentially more lucrative – but it has the added benefit of bringing the best creative writing from public toilets everywhere into print.

Well, my article didn't make the grade, but the lucky ones who did make it through paint a diverse picture of what we can expect come the year 2020. Of course, it may be a vision of 2020, but only time will tell whether it contains twenty-twenty vision. It is often ridiculous and, frankly, not the best stratagem for your trip to the bookies, but all human life is here. Quite a few forms of alien life, as well.

Most importantly, this is a book that had to be published now. Since, as one futurologist recently predicted, by the year 2020 no one will be able to read.

Enjoy.

Dave Gorman
London, 2003

The Soft Served World: Beyond the Internet

by Douglas Adams (U42)

Let's look a long way out for a moment.

What I would like to feel we have built, fifty or a hundred or two hundred years from now, is a soft model of the world. The Dataside of the world – for those who remember back to the early days of Starship Titanic. A database of the world. So that every object in the real world has its counterpart in the soft world. Except that every object in the soft world has a wealth of information attached to it – what it is, how it works, what its history is, what people think of it, what their experience of it is and the myriad

every object in the real world has its counterpart in the soft world

ways in which it is connected to the billions of other objects in the soft world.

In the real world, if you want to know what the view from the top of the Eiffel Tower looks like, you have to go there. In the soft world you can ask the Guide to show you what it looks like from the top of the Eiffel Tower. Maybe it can show you the view through a webcam there. Or maybe it can construct a virtual reality view for you in real time based on everything it knows about everything that can currently be seen from the top of the Eiffel Tower.

And, as you look down at your virtual view, you ask it how many of the cars you can see from your current vantage point are British. For a moment you think it's not working. Then you say, okay, how many of them are Peugeots? The view lights up with thousands of moving dots. Okay, how many of the cars you can see are currently playing Bach on their in-car stereos? A few dozen. Oh, there's one playing your favourite recording of the Schübler preludes. Does she have her flag up? Yes! She'll talk to you – but only because the only thing you'd asked about her was what she was listening to. Anything else and her flag would have been down for you. You chat for a bit about the music and quickly discover a tremendous rapport.

What about having dinner together? Okay... but she has a gluten problem, which restricts where she can eat. And you like turbot. A couple of restaurants light up in the view. One of them looks great for a romantic tryst, lots of alcoves and dim lighting. But some of the people who've eaten in there tonight have left notes saying that they're obviously understaffed in the kitchen and the food has been coming out cold or reheated. The other place gets raves about the food, but it's a bit bright and noisy. You decide that good food is the thing to go for. Then you remember – damn! You're not actually in Paris. You're in New Delhi and got a bit carried away.

That's all right, says your new friend. I'm actually in Albuquerque.

Oh well. You go back to your day job, erecting advertising hoardings on Mars. Soft Mars, that is, which has recently been added to the Soft Solar System. It was quite an expensive project because you can't rely on millions of people feeding back millions of snippets of information every day, which is what keeps the Soft Earth going so well.

If you want to visit Soft Mars – which is either a fully immersive environment at your local Trumbullarama, or a lower res

one on your own headset – you can either pay for a pristine version or explore it for free and put up with all the billboards advertising new movies, such as *Being Douglas Adams* about people who pay for the experience of banging their heads on doors a lot. There's a lot of controversy about polluting Martian virtual space with ads, of course.

And so on and so on. One could go on like this for pages; I think it demonstrates that we have to think beyond what you can put on a web page.

©2001 Completely Unexpected Productions Ltd.
Reproduced by kind permission of the Estate of Douglas Adams.

The Hitchhiker's Guide To The Galaxy Entry On Earth In 2020 (A970076)

by spook (U183955) ✪✪✪✪

Still Mostly Harmless.

The Monarchy 2020 (A892550)

by Andrew (U210412) ✪✪✪✪

The death of the popular Queen Elizabeth II in 2015 was widely mourned. Flowers were left at the gates of the palace and during ten days of mourning the streets of London were lined with millions of people wishing to see the coffin lying in state. Heads of state from all over the world came to the funeral. A mourner summed it all up when she said, 'It's like the end of an era.' The Queen had never been the same since her husband, Prince Philip, who spent the last few years of his life in a mental institution, died in 2009.

This has since proved to be a turning point for the monarchy. Prince Charles was declared King George VII, but his short reign was widely unpopular, in particular, his marriage to Lady

attempts to improve the popularity of the monarchy met with little success

Sandra Jackson, 30 years his junior. Her comments on working people, calling them sub-human, had provoked a barrage of criticism in the press during their courtship.

The reaction and the public outcry had been worse than Prince William's 'coming out' five years before at the annual dinner of an AIDS charity. Now living in Brazil with his life partner, he has distanced himself from the rest of his family after renouncing his claim to the succession. He will be disappointed though that sales of his book, *Diana: Memoirs of my Mother*, have failed to live up to expectations.

Five years on, subsequent attempts by St James's Palace to improve the popularity of the monarchy have met with little success, with only 5 per cent of people currently supporting the monarchy. After the Democratic Party's victory in the recent election, and their promise of a referendum, it seems that it is only a matter of time before the monarchy and a thousand years of tradition will be brought to an end.

The point of no return was the transformation of the M25 ring road into a private club

Posh Revolution
(A985403)
by letoph (U219058) ✪✪✪✪

Reuters Newswire
21 February 2020

This morning the UK Government announced the official break-up of England. The 'Posh Revolution' has happened. England will be devolved into two countries on 1 January 2021. London, Surrey and Buckinghamshire will form 'Middleshire'. The remaining English counties will remain in a new and smaller England.

The government and parliament will be transferred to Manchester. Both countries will be represented in all international organisations, with the significant difference that only Middleshire will have a seat on the UN council. After Brazil, England is the second nation to be broken up in such a manner.

King William has not yet announced which nation he favours. Royal pundits believe that, because he is deeply attached to Cornwall, he is likely to remain King of England, although he will keep his properties in Middleshire.

It all started in the winter of 2009, when high profile bankers in the City threatened to move their offices to Miami unless their high income tax rate was decreased to 20 per cent. Their arguments were simple. On the grounds that they didn't use public transport, sent their children only to public schools and private universities, didn't use the services provided by the NHS and were never unemployed, they should pay less tax than their co-citizens who partake in such activities. Once this first concession was allowed, every new year saw the diminution of the English state's prerogatives, through hardcore negotiations.

The point of no return was the transform-ation of the M25 ring road into a private club last year, with entry fees in excess of £200,000 and an annual concession between £20,000 and £100,000. This motorway therefore became the longest and largest luxury private road in the world. The idea has since been copied in Silicon Valley, Cape Town, Nice and all over Switzerland.

On a practical level, in order to become a citizen of Middleshire, applicants need to earn a minimum of £1m per year, have an asset of at least £10m and provide three referees within the so-called 'Group 1200'. Citizens of England who still work in Middleshire will be required to provide a 'laisser-passer' for their daily trips. All three political parties have expressed their admiration of the wealthy individuals who have decided, for moral reasons, to remain citizens of England.

Using modern genetic science, Buckingham Palace intends to clone Her Majesty, the late Queen Elizabeth, the Queen Mother. A spokes-person for the Palace has told the BBC: 'Her Majesty the Queen Mother was the last Royal everyone loved. She represented the highest attributes of duty and honour and of course single-handedly won us the Second World War. To this day we still remember with affection how Her Majesty stayed in London during the Blitz with only a steel reinforced bunker under Buckingham Palace to take shelter in, which she did with great courage. This is the Royal the British people want. It is time to bring back our favourite granny.'

Benjamin Briton (U210352)

Mullet Brings Hope (A932186)
by Carla Todd (U215464)

Having been consigned to the annals of history as a mockery of all that is good and glorious, 2020 finally sees the mullet command respect on a hitherto unknown scale as it is heralded as the next great hope for world peace.

Long has the mullet been mocked and its advocates lambasted – from the shame-faced growths of the infamous 'Aussie Mullets' in the mid-eighties (including the spin-off 'Permullet'), to the crazy heyday of the 'Billy Ray', made infamous by that last bastion of ill-fitting denim, Billy Ray Cyrus. Certainly, the mullet has done itself no favours! Not even the fairer sex was exempt from this follicle faux pas, as the 'Femullet' (or 'Fullet', as it came to be known) proved.

So very, very wrong, the majority concurred. So why the amazing turn-around in fortunes for this pariah of the preened?

Having discovered in 2017 that the mullet caused two very strong and opposing reactions – revulsion and hilarity – a team of eminent scientists have been researching ways in which the mullet could be genetically engineered to trigger the hilarity response alone. It was hoped that these properties of mirth could

Long has the mullet been mocked and its advocates lambasted

be developed to cure the terminally depressed, humourless and bitter.

Headed by the eccentric but brilliant Doctor X, the team based at the Institute of Mulletology in Geneva finally got a break-through early this year.

Having successfully grafted a mullet onto a laboratory mouse (since dubbed 'Billy Ray' by the lab technicians), the Institute carried out a series of con-trolled tests whereby the aforementioned terminally depressed, humourless and bitter were exposed to the mullet mouse whilst enduring a series of stressful, frustrating and depressing tasks. A mere one per cent of those test-ed failed to achieve feelings of immense peace and joy at the sight of little Billy Ray and his glossy bonce of brotherhood.

The government is confident that a new breed of 'Animullets' can be used not only as an effective replacement to Prozac but also as a source of universal joy and harmony which it is hoped will bring about world peace.

British Idyll – The Good Life? (A981696)

by Mad Maggie (U220038) ✪✪✪✪

Gwenglish, the new national language of 2020 United Kingdom, simplifies spelling and combines English, Welsh and Gaelic. No need for different road signs nowadays.

Private ownership of motor vehicles is outlawed except for essential service vehicles. These are powered by electricity. Horses are back in use for ambulances, fire engines and police vehicles. The bicycle is the chosen method of transport for most people. There are no petrol-based fuels. North Sea gas has now run out and all impor-tation of petroleum has ended since the American/British armies set ablaze the Gulf oil wells.

Allotments provided by the local council are again back in fashion for growing vegetables. Vegetables and soft fruit are grown by all garden owners, as importation from abroad has now ceased since the last climactic Gulf War.

Meat is strictly rationed and heavily taxed except for ostrich, emu and venison bred in large local farms. Fish farms flourish in all coastal regions and some progress has been made in developing many highly nutritious new species.

People are fitter and healthier as a result of working in their allotments, cycling everywhere and from the low cholesterol, high fibre diet.

There is no retirement age. Work is for life but it rarely involves more than two days per week so there is ample leisure time. Interest in all forms of participatory sport has dramatically increased along with the use of vast govern-ment-sponsored sports centres and swimming pools.

Utopia? Well, it seems that way. We can do anything, go anywhere, be anyone, and be extremely good at everything. I've scored goals in cup finals, won Snooker championships, performed at the Royal Albert Hall, made love to every fantasy lover you can imagine, been to other planets, killed, died, even worked. Think about every fantasy you've ever had and you'll catch my drift. It was no Utopia. People stopped going out, socialising and having relationships. Why trust reality when the fantasy world is perfect?

Jerry Gordon (U213513)

The Pop Charts Top Ten (A867549)

by Dr E Vibenstein (U40285) ✪✪✪

Sunday 8th November 2022
Here's this week's rundown of the most popular downloads appearing on an mp9 player near you...

1 The Beatles – 'Roll With It' Despite the legal arguments, the Beatles release their first single in 26 years and unveil their controversial new line-up: Noel, Liam, Darius and Ringo.

2 The Beckham Brothers – 'Ooh Baby I Need Your Loving' Seventh consecutive hit for Brooklyn and Romeo, the country's favourite footballing vocal duo.

3 Tom Jones & The Neuro Brothers – 'My Name Is' Pop's sprightliest octogenarian breathes new life into an old hit by forgotten turn-of-the-millennium rapper Eminem.

4 The Compo Boys – 'Heaven Is A Half Pint' Still at the front of the Yorkshire gangsta rap scene after ten years, the Compo Boys return with another eulogy to extreme violence and real ale.

5 The Charlotte Church Experience – 'Ooh Baby I Need Your Loving' On the eve of her farewell tour, Charlotte and the boys deliver another hard rock anthem, from the soundtrack of the movie *Beavis And Butthead: The Next Generation*.

6 The Stone Roses – 'Fools Gold (2022 Remix)' Following the tragic incident last month, in which Ian Brown was mauled by a pack of genetically engineered monkeys, the band's original label sees another marketing opportunity. This new mix becomes the band's biggest hit since 'Fools Gold (2018 Remix)'.

7 The Rolling Stones – 'Not Fade Away 2022' The first hit single to use the controversial new BTG (Beyond The Grave) technology to record the paranormal contributions of the late Stones, with additional overdubs by the only surviving member, the medical phenomenon that is Keith Richards.

8 S Club Seniors – 'Ooh Baby I Need A Nice Cup Of Tea And A Sit Down' With S Club Embryos poised to enter next week's chart, the original S Club line-up reforms, now with a combined age of 315.

9 Bob The Builder – 'Anarchy In The UK' It's hard to believe now, but the bad boy of rock started his career as a children's entertainer, before his much publicised alcohol and drug problems. Now a fully fledged thorn in the side of the establishment, Bob returns to the chart with his first release since 2020's 'Holidays In Cambodia'.

10 Status Quo – 'Rocking All The Way To The Bank' Oh no, not again.

Don't miss the entire top 300 rundown in 'Pick Of The Pops' with Alan Freemanoid, Sunday at 5 p.m. on BBC Radio 26.

Mother of a Nation is the story of Margaret Thatcher - spanning the time between her appointment as Prime Minister to her eventual downfall. Critics, who have seen dress rehearsals, have been unanimous in their praise for the musical. Much of which has been for Madonna for her brilliant portrayal of Margaret Thatcher - a strong, determined lady who sacrifices her own happiness for the good of her country. There has been some minor criticism about the historical accuracy of the plotline involving the brief, passionate, but ultimately doomed love affair between her and Ronald Reagan, played by Robert Smith, but, on the whole, critics have been warmly enthusiastic about this feel-good musical.

Johnnyp73 (U221156)

Brit Awards 2020: Nominations (A931817)

by turnipguru (U214759) ✪✪✪✪

Best Male Artist
▼ Sir Robert Williams
▼ Elton John (Part III)
▼ artificial intelligence 64
▼ 'The artist formally known as Darius'
▼ Brooklyn Beckham

This is hotly tipped to go to artificial intelligence 64 with his robotic anthem, 'even circuits bleed'.

Best Band
▼ Radiohead X
▼ The Clone Beatles
▼ Death From the Stars
▼ Not-So-Solid Crew
▼ Summersalt

Not-So-Solid Crew's 'Now We're Older' is a sentimental forty-something coming-of-age album favoured by many.

Best Album
▼ Now 86 (Various)

▼ The Galaxy Is Not Enough: OST
▼ Now We're Older: Not-So-Solid Crew
▼ Back Pain: Jordan
▼ Photographed Childhood: Brooklyn Beckham

Now 86 has been this year's hottest release.

Best International Artist
▼ Elvis
▼ Madonnatron
▼ Chi-aka-amundi
▼ Holly
▼ Prisoner #5845452

Elvis, a fantastic return to form (and life).

The Brit Awards 2020 promises to be a star-studded glitzy event. Set 30 miles above Earth in the Sting Memorial Astrodome, Davina McCall and the hologram of Parkinson present.

In 2020 I confidently expect the musical We Will Rock You still to be playing to packed, ecstatic houses in London and elsewhere, and the critics still to be wondering how they got it so wrong!!! — ha ha!

Brian May (U221383)

GOOD NEWS TV (A965487)

BY STUART BAKER-BROWN (U216531) ✪✪✪✪

In June 2020 the BBC will be celebrating the tenth year of their Good News programme. Over the years the popularity of Good News TV has grown and grown. Good News TV concentrated on good and positive news stories that have happened around the world, rather than the demoralising tales of woe that appeared on our television screens for many years.

A BBC spokesperson said, 'Ten years ago we realised that the public had finally had enough of all the unhappiness portrayed on their television screens, especially the news, but now we are managing to show the public that all is not darkness and doom. Good News TV has lifted the hearts of the viewing public and proved that the human race is not all bad.'

He added, 'I'm so glad we are in our tenth year. The public were fed up with all the sadness reported by our news teams. We knew we had to pull something out of the bag and stop the public from turning off their TV sets altogether. When it was decided that Good News TV was to go on air, we knew immediately that it would help to improve ratings and bring a smile back to the BBC's viewing public.'

Rebecca Brown, producer of the programme, said, 'We can only continue to unite rather than divide and prove to all that there is love and caring all over the world, rather than the death and destruction that was constantly shown on our screens.'

Headlines

Labour-Conservative Coalition Loses More Seats to Lib Dems

Taiwanese Factory Wins Third 'Manufactured Pop Idol' Title

And for all you Londoners out there…

Central Line To Re-open Friday

Bex (U221452)

The Universe 2020 (A938568)

by David H. Levy (U216309) ✪✪✪✪

When I was asked to write about what surprises the Universe might have in store by the year 2020, I thought how uncertain the prognosis for this endeavour might be. Had I been asked to write 20 years ago about the prospects for astronomical discovery before the year 2000, I would never for a minute have imagined that a comet would strike Jupiter or that the Hubble Space Telescope would yield images as gorgeous as the Pillars of Creation in Messier 16, the Eagle Nebula. So what follows is just one person's imagining of what might happen in the next 20 years.

1 The solar system and life

I suspect that the focus of astronomical discovery in the solar system will centre around Jupiter's moon Europa, Saturn's moon Titan and the outer solar system. Europa's ocean, hidden under a thick layer of ice, might yield some evidence of primordial life. Titan, being the target of a spacecraft landing, will undoubtedly yield some of her amazing secrets. There is also a good possibility that primitive fossilized life forms, or possibly even active life forms, will be confirmed on Mars, providing some real evidence that life exists on other planets.

2 The deep sky

We are so far overdue for a supernova in our own galaxy that I'll go out on a limb and predict that the next one could be found in the next 20 years. It might be hidden behind clouds of interstellar dust, which would diminish its brightness, or it may shine as a blazing star – as bright as the other three supernovae that have been recorded in our own galaxy in 1054, 1572 and 1604. The 1054 supernova was visible in broad daylight for almost a month.

As galaxies are being discovered farther and farther away in space and time, I suspect that we will see examples of galaxies formed not long after the Universe itself was formed. With each discovery of an older galaxy, we go closer in time to the actual formation of the Universe.

3 Greater international cooperation in astronomy

I predict also that over the next 20 years there will be a far greater cooperation among nations in science,

and particularly in astronomy. Astronomers in many countries will share their observations, ideas, knowledge and opinions. And that might be the greatest development of all.

The USE (United States of Europe) have solved the problem of over-sensitive robots in space by genetically engineering gerbils to make very small astronauts. Robots fitted with artificial intelligence have been sent into deep space on survey missions, only to send messages back to Earth complaining that they are lonely, and can Mission Control read them a story, and incidentally, the TV reception is lousy, and what's with all the Des O'Connor CDs...?

Banalitycrow (U214773)

With each discovery of an older galaxy we go closer in time to the formation of the Universe itself

China: Over the Moon (A926822)
by Stewart Ryder (U213965) ✪✪✪✪

2020 heralds several landmarks in terms of human life beyond Earth's atmosphere. 2003 marked China's first real steps into the new space race when they successfully placed their first 'Taikonaut' in orbit. 2012 saw the completion of the Chinese Orbital Observatory for scientific experimentation involving prolonged human exposure to space. Seventeen years and several billion RenMinBi after the start of their manned space programme, China is the first nation trying to build a permanent manned science station on the lunar surface. Its main purpose: to research the possible use of the Moon's primary resources of titanium, aluminium and silicon for the production of solar cells and establish whether further stations, primarily production facilities, can be built safely and efficiently.

The six-man team, due to launch in June, will spend 150 days away from Earth utilising the pre-delivered payloads to construct the living habitat and setting up the huge solar garden to supply the lunar habitat's power needs. The June date is later than initially planned due to the loss of one of the solar cell payloads that exploded minutes after take-off.

The Chinese hope that, with continual research into lunar production facilities and spatial manufacturing processes, the first lunar community could reach the launch pad as early as 2028. This will coincide with the sending into space of the youngest human at the age of 18, as well as the birth of the first baby conceived in space. The infant's good health will be a promising start for man's future presence on other planets.

China's space pioneering is an added blow to early Western beliefs that predicted the rise in 'space tourism' and a move away from government-controlled space programmes. The World Economy Implosion of 2008 ended the period of prosperity that had promised to see the commercial space interests of the Western world flourish resulting in a hiatus for all future NASA and ESA missions. Now, unable to obtain any government funding due to increased economic pressures and a slow recovery, it seems that the West may have to watch the Chinese disappear into the great beyond.

The only planned event of consequence for Western and Russian space interests in 2020 is the removal of the International Space Station from orbit. Having been abandoned in 2016, the once promising international venture will meet a fiery end when it is steered into a decaying orbit and crashed into the Pacific to join its predecessor, the equally ill-fated Mir station, at the bottom of the ocean.

Fat Tax (A935813)
by Jimmi (U215605) ✪✪✪

Health and beauty in 2020 is big business, but not in the way you would expect. After several manufactured pop artists were found dead, drowned in toilet bowls with fingers down the backs of their throats, a novel health craze started. With cries of 'Bulk up!' and 'Big is Beautiful!', people were encouraged to eat more and more.

The newly liberated masses greedily gorged their appetites. Food was shovelled into gaping mouths. The nation ballooned. At one point, walking down the high street became akin to

The under-educated and overfed instantly became the seriously rich

travelling amidst a group of obese baboons. Something had to be done.

It was then that the Fat Farms appeared. These small, unobtrusive buildings sprung up in all our major cities. 'What are these?' we asked

ourselves, and then the queues appeared: long lines of the fat, gross and bulbous members of society. They walked in one door corpulent chunks of wobbling flesh, and out the other side they emerged deflated. The Fat Farms were buying the fat, sucking the putrid yellow mush out, and selling it as high quality soap.

Fat was now worth its weight in gold. Fat people were now the fat cats. The under-educated and overfed instantly became the seriously rich. This, understandably, made the rest of us extremely jealous.

We elected a new 'Old Labour' government, whose plan to redistribute wealth, and indeed weight, revolved on the introduction of a new tax. Pay As You Eat (P.A.Y.E.) was brought in, charging individuals directly for the mass of food they consume. Now none of us can be fat; we cannot afford to be. We are a nation of stick-insects, but we do have a lot of nice soap!

Future Super-Men (A972623)
by Dr Ian Banks (U219750) ✪✪✪✪✪

'Do my pecs look big in this shirt?' he asked, contemplating the £2,000 he paid for implants.

'Yes, of course they do,' his third wife replied for the umpteenth time. 'Now if you don't mind I have to catch the 9.15 flight to LA.' He glanced over the TV headlines as he poured out GM cereal for his young children: 'President Bruce Willis Denies Canadian Incursion Over Rapeseed Oil Fields'. Like all men of his age, he routinely checked the mail for his call-up papers. 'Maybe I'll fail the medical.'

Throwing back the testosterone reductase inhibitor pill and the lipid uptake blocker, he patted himself once on his full head of hair and twice on his six pack. Unlikely, he grimaced, given the compulsory checks imposed by the NHS. 'Damn things cost me more than my monthly depilation,' he muttered, rubbing his baby smooth chin.

Feeling completely miserable, he checked his waist to height ratio, examined his testicles and stuck the prostate checker up his backside, wincing ever so slightly as the hormone sampler took its tiny drop of blood. 'I'm going to need new testosterone patches,' he complained, ripping the old one off his hairless thigh.

Bang on cue, the baby started crying. 'It's fine for her,' he mumbled, 'swanning off on budget airline trips to the States or Free

the anti-impotence nasal sprays were fine, but they didn't help his declining sperm count

Iraq under military escort, while I'm stuck at home looking after the kids with only *The Big Un's Vintage Clips* to look forward to on the telly.'

Warming the feed bottle gave him time to think about his sex life. Yes, the anti-impotence nasal sprays were fine, but they didn't help his declining sperm count. And the fact that the same thing was happening to all European men didn't stop him feeling

that his manhood was slipping away. Rolling a spliff helped lift his mood.

Not even the government health warning on the packet could dent his enjoyment of Afghanistan Blam. His vision was not so bad and with his laser keratotomy he could even see the wart on Euan Blair's nose as he addressed the Labour Party Conference. 'What would I like most for the seasonal event formerly known as Christmas,' he pondered through a pleasant haze, 'a new electric car or a nose job?' Decisions, decisions.

Perhaps the most important reason why we will stay fat is that the entire economy is based on 'image is everything', the popular soft drink maker's slogan. The body image is the biggest part of this industry. If there are no fat people, there would be no sensational product to sell. What is more profitable to advertise - a 'ThinQuick' bar or an apple? The economy needs fat people!

Ellie Mouliartchik (U215387)

Childhood - A Forgotten Concept? (A950393)

by taj1701 (U215861) ✪✪✪

Will there be 'natural' pregnancy in 2020? The time-honoured nine months? Eight months? Six months? Artificial wombs? Surrogacy? Amniocentesis? CVS, FSH, Nuchal Fold? The end of disability? The future of conformity? Elective

with egg and sperm donations, artificial wombs and artificial sperm, are parents a fashion accessory?

caesareans? Natural childbirth? Birthing baths? Acupuncture? Doula? Homebirth? Hospital birth? What will our babies eat? Breast feed or bottle feed? The controversy increases.

Artificial breast milk, organic, additive-free, sugar-free, wet nurses, feed on demand, follow routine, for 2 weeks, for 6 weeks, for 18 weeks, for 8 years, who knows? Will mother care for them? Will she work full time? Will she work part time? Will she work at all? Career breaks, parental leave, childminders, crèches, nurseries, pre-schools, academies, work from home, teleworking, isolation, commute, guilt. Will father care for them? Is father needed? We have egg donation, sperm donation, artificial womb, artificial sperm. Is father a fashion accessory? Is mother? Or will grandparents care as old age is pushed further away?

Have the injections, don't have the injections? MMR, XYZ, never ending. Triple vaccine, quadruple vaccine? On and on. Fear of strangers, fear of disease, beware the paedophiles, beware cable TV, parental locks, watch TV, don't watch TV, play computer games, don't play computer games, beware car fumes, childhood asthma, car seats, pension at birth, mortgage forever, fear of holocaust, 6 billion people, planet exploding, antibacterial, sanitary, convenient, clean, boring.

Fun? What's that? A forgotten word? Joy? Nature? Happiness? Exploration? Where will be the wonder of exploration? A constant rush to 'improve' and conform.

Childhood 2020 – a forgotten concept, too?

I think the best the council could do is to send out a note to all army chiefs saying 'STOP WAR' so no more lives are lost. They should use the old war planes to build electrical equipment for the poor people in other parts of the world. The people in cities that don't like any other city should get to know each other better.

Stitches, aged 8 (U221324)

I think that the world will never be peaceful and that no countries will be able to make a peace treaty. Because, to be honest, if this is what is happening now and there is no way of stopping it, what is there to be happy about in the future?

Liam Seals, aged 11 (U213606)

A Day in the Life of a 2020 GP [A863633]

by Dr Trisha Macnair (U207898) ✪✪✪✪

The alarm goes off early and I leap into action, as I have a vid-cam clinic before breakfast with the local elderly-care facility. A prolonged drop in the birth rate since the 1970s means that the old now far outnumber the young. So although I'm 62, I must work until I drop.

The cost of looking after so many elderly people has put a huge strain on the

> **we vaccinate against so many things now, including cancer and even drug addiction**

health service. In order to cut costs, the government can now forcibly detain and treat people for smoking, addiction, obesity, or any other condition that leads to huge medical bills. Worse still for those sad souls who slip towards dementia – caring for them is considered a waste of precious funds and they can be legally eased into the afterlife with a quick shot of opiates.

The clinic is over quickly. On-site biosensors controlled by staff at the home have done half of the diagnoses before I even hook up to speak to the residents, and the standard treatment protocols on their computer explain how their medical problems should be managed. I often wonder why a doctor is needed at all!

After breakfast, two emergency vid-cam consults call in. The first is a young boy who may have measles, but it's hard to be sure. Fears about the MMR vaccine at the turn of the century led to a major epidemic and many deaths, after which vaccination rates returned to an all-time high. I explain to his mother how to check for the measles virus at the local diagnostic pharmacy, where they can then buy anti-viral drugs. One benefit of the long years of war was the rapid development of anti-infective medicines.

Then I sift through my email. It's the usual round of press releases including an invite to a lecture called 'Cancer: an extinct killer?'. Most cancers can now be rapidly treated using genetic switch modifiers – treatments that simply switch off the genetic signals that trigger tumours.

The afternoon is spent in the vaccination clinic, where I receive an urgent warning about the long-anticipated flu pandemic. I immediately email all my patients to come in for jabs. We vaccinate against so many things now, including cancer and even drug addiction. Some conditions still plague us, especially heart disease which remains the number one killer.

I finish the day by logging on to my online educational programme and completing my monthly evaluation assignment at the General Medical Council's website. I download the results of my weekly DNA screening test which checks my genes, watching out for up to 648 different diseases, and then it's lights out.

Re: A Day in the Life of a 2020 GP
I am in awe at Dr Macnair's Orwellian attitude as regards forced treatment and euthanasia. It just won't happen. Can you imagine the enormous social pressure that would rise against even the suggestion of such laws? Even she might think twice if it were her mother or father being eased into the afterlife.
Augurist (U214438)

2020 – I've Just Gotten Older (A934274)

by Slartibartfast (U213135) ✪✪✪✪

I admit I'm known as a bit of a sceptic. I'd like to believe that we'll all have interactive fridges and household pets which also double as vacuum cleaners, but I will stake my life on the belief that very little will have changed in the year 2020.

I remember watching a video on *Blue Peter* where they showed a few school children in the 1970s or 80s saying what they thought the world would be like in the year 2000. I can honestly say that I was astonished by how advanced they believed we would be.

These are the people who will be running the country in years to come, so let's hope that they wise up as to how long it actually takes to change something. People take comfort in similarity, with change usually greeted with scepticism and even fear. When will we feel 'comfort' in the fact that change is for the better, and that development doesn't necessarily mean jumping in head first?

It's sad to think that we'll be having the same problems in 17 years' time. The idea that we still won't know how to programme our

even if a mobile phone is the size of a matchbox...doesn't mean that it's useful

media players to tell the time or understand how to use the Internet effectively can be quite depressing. Although I do believe that technology will continue to get smaller and smaller in an attempt to show how intelligent we all are. This is until people realise that small objects are very easy to lose, and even if a mobile phone is the size of a matchbox it still doesn't mean that it's useful.

Why, when we are able to send a man to the Moon, are we now concentrating on building weapons of mass destruction? I know that it's not a simple matter of ridding the world of killer viruses, nuclear devices and other really nasty bits of weaponry.

We have a lot more to discover and learn. Let's not get hung up on blowing to bits the person who disagrees with us. Let's take the steps needed to change this world for the better, before global warming or nuclear war catch up with us. I don't want to grow up in a world where science is second to war.

(One thing I would love to see is a Talkie Toaster, though.)

Futurologists are rarely right – predictions about the future are rarely more than the extrapolation of existing trends and cannot, by their nature, predict quantum shifts of invention or focus.

Therion Ware (U210356)

You can't change the past. We can change the present. The present will change the future. The future will not be changed by one man. It will not be changed overnight. There will be no miracle. No wonder of modern science. No asteroid. No life on Mars. The future will be what we make it. Whether we make it good or evil rests solely on our shoulders.

MonsAltus (U213825)

In 17 years time, 2020, I shall be my parents.

John Newby (U215104)

Small Steps, Not Giant Leaps (A930304)

by Robert Tye (U185318) ✪✪✪✪

I was browsing the BBC website the other day and decided to take a look at some of the archives, when I stumbled across a section written in 2003 about what the world would be like in 2020. So I decided to look through and write an article on the differences between what people thought would happen and what actually happened.

Let's start with science and technology. The overwhelming idea from the articles was that today in 2020, we would be hugely more advanced than we were 20 years ago. Well, to a certain extent we are. The proliferation of computers today is far greater than it was 20 years ago, and with most of the adults today coming from a generation that grew up with computers, people are generally a lot more computer literate. The computers are also much faster. Twenty years ago the maximum commercial processor speed was about three GHz, but today you are looking at more like 30.

There are, however, no signs yet of 3D interactivity, and so we are still confined to using two dimensions. And although phones these days are much more advanced, people don't really use them for major computing, preferring instead to use an actual keyboard. The idea of talking to the computer was nice, until it was realised that it was far too noisy in the office.

The combustion engine is still in use, although somewhat more efficient than 20 years ago, topping around 70 miles to the gallon. Most cars are hybrids – also able to run on electricity.

The idea of living on the Moon or Mars was nice. But after the Mars mission of 2012 (in which it was determined that terra-forming the Mars landscape would take too long, and running supplies to colonies on Mars was impractical) the idea of colonising was scrapped. We continue to use robotic probes for exploration.

Lastly, I decided to take a look at the progress we have made in medicine. The whole world rejoiced in 2007 as the cure for AIDS was developed and administered to millions around the world. However, other superbugs were soon to follow. Many forms of cancer now have a cure, but many still remain untreatable and fatal.

The greatest advancement has to be in genetic research. After the genome was successfully mapped, many gene therapies were developed, allowing the treatment of many genetic disorders by replacing the faulty DNA. The screening of embryos to stop the development of babies with fatal genetic diseases has cut child mortalities drastically.

Well, that is my round-up of things today as opposed to 20 years ago. I wonder what things will be like in another 20 years.

after the Mars mission of 2012... the idea of colonising was scrapped

The Future Is Today (A986907)

by Andrew Pinder (U221200) ✪✪✪

One of my colleagues has a metal plaque on his kitchen wall from Matt Groening's marvellous TV cartoon show *Futurama*, a story of animated life in the thirtieth century. It states boldly: 'The future is today. Worry about it tomorrow!' There's probably more than a modicum of truth in it.

Whenever people turn their minds to the future, inevitably they conjure up one of two scenarios: apocalyptic or Utopian. In reality, of course, it's likely to be a mix of the two. And personally, I'm rooting for more of the latter.

My view concerns the relationship between citizen and government. That sounds grand, but it means me and you. How we interact. How the machinery of government responds to our needs. How our lives are made easier – or more difficult.

Government will be less something that is done to us, and more something that we are part of. Our sense of community will be different, too. We'll be part of many different networks forming and re-forming around different interests and needs.

Traditional organisations, including governments, are vertical hierarchies. The networked society, and the networked government

> **the internet will be seen...in the same way as gas and electricity**

which serves it, will be organised much more horizontally. At the heart of our future is mobility, but not in the conventional geographic sense. Information will travel and information will connect people.

So here are some of Pinder's Predictions – to be taken with more than a pinch of salt:

▼ The Internet will reach everyone. It will be seen as a utility – in the same way we view gas or electricity. An essential service, but one that is not thought about.

▼ Personal information will not be the 'hot potato' it is today. It will be essential in providing tailored services.

▼ Government will be able to address everyone at a personal level, and vice versa. Democracy will be enhanced.

▼ Government will learn to be more responsive. More voices will be heard – not just the loudest ones.

▼ Government will be more accountable. Knowledge is power, and there will be a shift away from central-isation. IT is a great leveller and cascades down, not up.

▼ Convergence will be a thing of the past. IT will be as commonplace as the cell phone. Just another tool for everyday life, used by grannies and teenagers alike.

▼ 'e' will lose its mystique, because it will be part of everything we do. Remember how 'colour' used to be the prime descriptor for television?

Voting Rights (A934814)

by Chris Skinner (U210468) ✪✪✪✪

The annual government token vote was up for renewal. Was it worth voting? Who cared?

She had voted every year, but the vote made no difference. She was a rare and unusual breed – one of only a few who bothered. Although the technological innovations of the last few years had made voting as easy as pressing the 'enter' button on a keyboard, most could not be bothered or were too frightened to bother. After all, the government could easily identify who voted for whom from their master database and this often meant more frequent visits from the transaction police. That factor alone prohibited many from voting.

Her friends had become so cynical about their leadership: their ineffectual ability to change anything and the rumours of secretive payments to policymakers who twist and shape policies in the direction of the corporate lobbyists. The combined effect had made them all believe that government was a waste of their time.

The now archaic twentieth-century principles of democratic power are being rapidly replaced by the corporate twenty-first century's enormous pecuniary power.

In 2020 Britain there is no voting anymore – only investing.

M. J. Blank (TU217285)

The networked media did not help. The continual headlines about power brokers in government being caught in comprising positions – from sex to money to greed to pure stupidity – had left no one above reproach within the governmental corridors.

The only governments that anyone took note of were far removed from the individual. Their nation followed a regional superpower, which, in turn, followed the other regional superpowers in order to reap the rewards of the commercial opportunities offered by them. The whole thing was a circle of money generated for commerce and power.

So what did she care?

Well, she cared a lot. She always voted. She felt she could make a difference. She was one of the 10 per cent of people in the country who bothered.

But she felt she had to. After all, she was the Head of State in charge of government.

most could not be bothered or were too frightened to bother

learning

TOMORROW'S SCHOOL (A864407)
BY LIBBY (U207769) ✪✪✪✪

Education will probably not improve in the next 20 years. Bleak? Perhaps, but if the return of a left-wing party, whose campaign pledge was 'education, education, education', can't find a way of improving both students' and teachers' experiences of learning, who is going to?

The proposed solutions have an emphasis on technology and e-learning – using high-tech gadgets and broadband connections to try to raise an iota of interest in students about learning.

Between now and 2020, it seems unlikely that such an expensive solution will really be implemented. The prospect of war and economic downturn has always meant that education is put off for another few years. And funding is so overdue that the returns of a fully supportive government will not be visible for a while. However, there is another way.

In 2020, schools will have smaller class sizes and a higher teacher to student ratio. Students will be free to study chosen topics and set their own projects from the age of 10. Older students will mentor younger students, taking pressure off teachers in some areas. Standardised tests and multiple pre-university qualifications will be thrown out along with mandatory PE. (Woo hoo!) But how will we achieve this Utopian state of learning? Not with computers, but with hard lessons.

Education is not a right. Anyone who wants to be

THE KEY QUESTION IS, 'WHAT IS THE PURPOSE OF EDUCATION?'

educated has the right to an opportunity, but the hard cold reality is that you cannot educate someone who doesn't want to be. High-tech learning is a tool in the hands of those that want to learn, and a novelty in the hands of those who don't.

Besides, technology will have to advance to artificial intelligence levels to be able to react to the individual needs of students. And, let's face it, wouldn't it be easier for everyone involved if people who didn't want to be there weren't there at all?

Newcomers or those returning to education will need to know basic oral and written English and basic maths. Those with anti-social behaviour will choose whether to attend special sessions or to opt out of academic education.

Students cannot learn if they don't feel safe and well; this is accepted knowledge. So why allow bullies to ruin a class, a year or a pupil's life?

The key question that needs answering in the next 20 years is, 'What is the purpose of education?' If it is merely a method of acquiring a 'good' (high-paying) job – a means of curbing independent thought and behaviour, creating an apathetic, morally ambiguous, reward-seeking and shallow nation of consumers, then we're on the right track.

Welcome to the Educasium (A940268)

by Phil M (U216394) ✪✪✪✪

I am delighted to have this chance to welcome you to our wonderfully resourced Educasium and hope that your time with us will be as profitable as we can make it. As you scroll down this screen, you will surely be amazed by what we have to offer. By following a few simple guidelines, the Intro Mark II will be able to select the appropriate course for you, and will introduce you to your tutors. At the same time, the Student Mentor PX8 will be assessing your needs and will be formulating a specially-tailored version of our highly acclaimed pastoral programme. This will be available to you from the moment you have accepted your ID strip. You will also be reassured to know that the Well Scholar 425 has scanned your body, and a print-out of your past, current and potential future illnesses is available to you at the Medical Centre workstation. Please use this facility discreetly, as it is often over subscribed – especially during examination weeks.

Once you leave this terminal, you should make your way down the cyber-posted route towards the Knowledge Accumulation Suite, where the Educatron 2020 will introduce itself and start you on your individual induction programme. We can now offer you a variety of interplay scenarios ranging from gruffly efficient to avuncular and friendly.

Here at the college we pride ourselves in the number and quality of our staff. Bi-monthly visits are a regular feature of our courses, so you can expect to see someone several times during your stay with us.

Need to call on someone personally in an emergency? Ask yourself if your Student Mentor cannot deal with the situation. They are surprisingly well-versed in student problems and will offer the soundest

the Educatron 2020 will introduce itself and start you on your individual induction programme

advice on almost all subjects, however delicate. In fact, the PX8 has the enviable reputation of being one of the best Education Mentors currently on the market.

In conclusion, I would like to wish you a happy and responsive time with us here at the Educasium, and trust that your programme of mental development will be to your advantage.

So log on and learn.

Statistics Vaguely Blurred (A950050)

by Ed Sparks (U215529) ✪✪✪✪

I was thinking about writing an article for the 2050 Book of the Future. My mum says she did it when she was my age. She made me laugh when she said that only 5 per cent of the articles made the grade! Mu-um! Who believes in percentages any more? She said it was all the rage back then. 'Damlise and statistics' she calls it.

Apparently, the aptly named Blur government used to use statistics to tell people how happy they were: 65 per cent were 10 per cent happier for 12 per cent more time than they had been before the Blur party came to power. And advertisers were 24 per cent more likely to use focus groups on 56 per cent of occasions for 35 per cent of clients' something-or-other. I asked, 'How did you get 35 per cent of a client?' Mum got sulky then and wouldn't answer.

Thank goodness the Vague years changed all that. It must have done their heads in, all them numbers. It would mine, but then they used to do something called maffs in schools back then. Yes, Prime Minister Vague did us all a favour getting rid of numbers. Not entirely of course; I mean, some people still use them, but they're not like us. The people who attend superversity don't even live in the same world as us normal graduates.

I mean, what's with them, right? Everybody gets a degree when they leave Gala Bingo University at 25, yeah? But them eggheads just aren't satisfied. Get this, they actually leave home to go and live in these weird communities called 'campers', in places like Durham and Cambridge and whatever.

Mum says they've got a 40 per cent better chance of being in the top 10 per cent of earners. I say, they're welcome to it. Who wants to be a damlise? Or a statistic? I'm glad I never had to learn about percentages. I'm quite happy being more or less all right about half the time and not so bad the rest. I reckon my guess is as good as the next and that most people think pretty much the same about the majority of stuff.

But will they think the same in 2050?

Prime Minister Vague did us all a favour getting rid of numbers

For most of the morning I am in the classroom with nearly 50 pupils, another consequence of the teacher shortage. Older colleagues, with whom I worked earlier in my career, would be surprised to see this, and more surprised still to learn that discipline has actually improved, despite the larger class sizes. But the reason for this is that since teachers were allowed to use a quick jolt of electricity, administered from the desk at the front of the room to those pupils who are disruptive or simply not paying attention, behaviour has improved markedly.

Kajira Roxanne (U214543)

Education, pop music and advertising will eventually blend into a whole new form of infomercials, geared first to appease an already struggling population, then to select those who would be useful 'employees'.

Researcher 217439

TWENTY SCHMENTY (A941429)

BY ARGONAUT (U215822)

Entertainment

In the year 2020, there will be more television channels than there are people to watch them. People will be required by law to watch at least 25 advertisements every day – not including advertisements for their own TV channels. Lifestyle gurus will be elevated to dictators, commanding nations and even entire continents. India will be run by Alan Titchmarsh and will be mostly decking with the odd water feature. Pop careers will be so short that music videos will have to be shot at 10,000 frames per second. The news will be read by convicts because they are cheaper.

Science & Technology

Computers will be so powerful that some of them will actually be useful, though this will be entirely by accident. The Internet will be so full of information that nobody can get a word in edgeways. Opera will be delivered in pill form, and people will be genetically engineered to find it interesting. Mobile phones will be the only other form of technology, and we will use them to cook, wash clothes, change tyres, remove stones from horses' hooves and deflect the blast from a nuclear assault.

Education

Reading out loud will be an A-Level subject.

Work

Most people will commute to work. The average journey time will be two hours each way, but the average distance travelled will be less than 50 metres in total. Nobody will walk anywhere because most of Britain will be under shark-infested waters. People will either answer the telephone in an annoying sing-song voice, send emails to each other or present reality TV shows for a living. These will be the only career options available in 2020.

War

The United States will continue to spend astronomical sums of money developing top-secret weapons that everybody knows about. The War Against Terror will have moved to the streets of Berwick-on-Tweed, which will be reduced to rubble by months of relentless carpet-bombing. A weapon will be invented that only kills bad people who deserve to die.

Alarm clocks haven't improved very much over the years – quite the opposite. Instead of letting you sleep like they used to do, your average alarm clock gets louder the longer you try to ignore it, squeals at you if you try to use the snooze button and won't respond to its off-switch until you're standing up when you press it.

MaW (U55669)

The Futurologist's Last Forecast (A998148)

by Jarmo (U221928) ✪✪✪✪

I always said the future would be full of fine ideas,
With plenty of inventions packing out my pensioned years:
From bio-engineered crops that combat acid rain,
To solar cars and high-tech bars with drinks that boost the brain.

I'd never have predicted that what people wanted most
Were robot slaves to cook and serve them sizzling cheese-on-toast,
Or dreamt a used-car salesman would design a better wheel,
And HRH would abdicate in favour of John Peel.

And (even mistranslated) Nostradamus never said
That one day every home would have a web-enabled bed,
Or could've guessed that old George Best would broker global peace,
As P.M. David Beckham's envoy in the Middle East.

But what shook me the most was when it became the height of chic
For stars to sculpt their lips into a plastic puffin's beak.
So there! I'll swear the future is too fickle to foresee,
And forecast I'll be forced instead to take up history.

But Will It Work? *(A985548)*

by Ian Pearson *(U221059)* ✪✪✪✪

The future will be very exciting, but not always for the reasons we expect. In just a few years, chips will be everywhere. This will be a very mixed blessing. Imagine eating jelly babies in 2010 and suppose Bassetts have redesigned them with embedded edible electronics. When you bite the head off the first one, it will scream and send a distress message to its friends. They could launch a virus attack on your home PC, trashing its hard drive. So eating jelly babies could become a blood sport, where the victims can fight back.

There will be chips in packaging to replace today's

bathrooms will have a smart toilet using the latest in bum recognition to identify you

barcodes, and our clothes will have chips that can be read by washing machines. All very well, but this means that products on supermarket shelves will be able to link to the shop's and manufacturer's web sites.

The clothes shop will recognise the tags in your clothes, enabling snotty teenage assistants to be sarcastic about how long you've been wearing the same jumper. Bottles of Coke might refuse loudly to share a trolley with Pepsi, or the Tesco Finest might sneer condescendingly at the Value orange juice you are buying. Shopping tantrums from kids are bad enough without stroppy products too.

Even when you get it home, the gadgets in your home will all be networked. The bathroom will have a smart toilet, using the latest in bum recognition to identify you. It will track your health and weight. If it decides to put you on a diet, the fridge might refuse to open, or the microwave might refuse to cook your breakfast. Kitchen rage will be widespread.

Our social lives will improve though. Already, there are badges for people to use in night-clubs to identify what sort of person they are looking for. In a few years, these badges will be able to hold all kinds of personal information, and you will be able to find someone both fully compatible and sufficiently desperate in the first minute. If they don't look as attractive as you hoped, you can use your new active contact lenses to digitally remove their face from the field of view and substitute an image of your favourite fantasy figure.

A few years on from that and you will be able to have chips in your skin. Some will be displays, active tattoos, or will control active make-up (applied in front of a digital bathroom mirror), video nail varnish and context-dependent perfume. Others will link to your nervous system, allowing you to record sensations onto your computer and replay them at will. You could send your partner an orgasm by email when you are away on a business trip.

Now imagine if it all goes wrong. And it will sometimes. However smart the technology becomes, it will sometimes fail. And the fancier the technology, the more spectacular will be the result of its failure.

Year 2020 Song
(A941528)

by StuWil84 (U216012)

Wide screen TV fills the wall of my room,
I've got hologram pics of my house on the moon.
My cat is a robot and so is my son,
And the year 2020 has hardly begun.

My car flies as fast as that Concorde of old,
And alchemy means there's no shortage of gold.
The toaster's IQ is two hundred and three,
And the year 2020 is currency-free.

My laptop's so thin I can fold it in half;
In winter my phone doubles up as a scarf.
My modem's so quick it types faster than me,
The year 2020 is so full of glee.

Time is in metric, it's eighty past nine,
And grandma's in storage, pickled in brine.
Next week I'm going to get me a clone,
The year 2020's no fun on your own.

This is the end of this fabulous song,
I hope by now you're all singing along.
In seventeen years you will hopefully see,
The year 2020 is the place to be.

Intelligence not included? (A921764)

by Kev Jones (U213690) ✪✪✪

The Stockholm agreement in 2017 on the Universal Intelligence Interface gave rise to promises of labour-saving devices beyond imagination, electronic marketing assistants to filter the increasing bombardment of advertisements and not forgetting the Holy Grail, the electronic therapist.

However, three years on and the reality is that last night I came home to my toaster informing me that my television had become so frustrated with my failure to acknowledge that it had recorded an entire series of 'Friends' that all data had now been deleted.

Now don't take me for a teraphobe. I do appreciate the luxury of having 'intelligence shipped as standard' in most appliances (even if they still don't include batteries). I like my fridge to re-order the groceries when running low. Even the cat is getting used to the vacuum cleaner deciding it's time to clean.

However, for every stress-reducing feature that is introduced, it is another element of complexity in an already over-complex world. It is as though an eternal

even the cat is getting used to the vacuum cleaner deciding it's time to clean

race has started between the designer and consumer that neither can win. The designer's role is to conjure increasingly bizarre scenarios for engineers to programme appliances. Whilst these are intended to be stress-reducing features, consumers are spending an increasing amount of time (and stress) trying to fathom what the designers have changed while upgrading the microwave user-interface.

My kids now have to tell me that I can't use the garage door between 5 and 6 p.m. because it's downloading the latest security and safety patch. If my grandfather could hear that sentence he would consider the very notion preposterous. I don't blame creative designers or the intelligence chips or even my kids, but wouldn't it be a good thing if the next time you ordered a simple device it said 'quality design comes as standard, intelligence not included'?

By 2020, humans will be so technologically reliant that they will actually devolve. The future boy will be stumped by doors that have to be pushed open, perplexed by stairs that have to be walked up and baffled by foodstuffs that have to be cooked.

LJ Harrison (U215954)

The interesting thing about the future is that science and technology are racing ahead, probably at an ever-increasing pace. Yet human attitudes are barely changing. That makes forecasting the future difficult - technology has its foot on the accelerator and culture has its foot on the brake.

Dr B (U216555)

Tattoos with a Purpose (A944165)

by Eddie Smith (U201412) ✪✪✪✪

Body art, in the form of tattoos, has always had some kind of social meaning. The art of painting the body was originally a form of identification. When instinct ruled over conscience, tattoos were a self-proclamation of one's own strengths.

It wouldn't be unusual to assume that tattoos are, in a way, a rebellious tool. Over the last couple of decades, body art has seen an overwhelming increase in popularity, especially among women. Once, tattoos were purely in the domain of the male, mostly manual or unskilled workers, and followed pre-designed templates. Then, in the 1990s and Noughties, women of all ages adopted the idea of being tattooed as a symbol of 'girl power'.

However, the tattoos were so small, they were mostly hidden away from public during the day, shown just at night and only noticeable if the owner of the tattoo drew your attention to it. Even then, one would

dead or alive, marked bodies can be identified by their tattoos

have to zoom in to recognise the image.

But now there is a new kid on the block! From the depths of inner city Britain comes the 'marked body'. Dead or alive, marked bodies can be identified by their tattoos. Someone who has a marked body has every limb tattooed with their National Insurance number – arms, hands, legs, feet, torso, neck and head. Most hardcore citizens have their number painted on the side of the face along their lower jaw line. This is a message to others that their bodies are marked and traceable to their last known movements and so deters the usual attack or mugging.

This has prompted scientists to look into 'etching' numbers on bones. The purpose of this is to make skeletal remains traceable if the body is burnt beyond recognition, and tests involving microscopic high frequency erosion have proved to have encouraging results. If successful, this technique would go a long way to combat 'gangland body dumping' and 'cremation without consent'.

So, it seems tattoos are proving useful after all, and any efforts made to make our cities safer places to live should be commended.

By the way, if you find a 'clean' body without any tattoo of any sort, please get in touch with David Dickinson!

It is fantastic that already (in 1999) 14,464 prisoners were tagged and released early following the introduction of the Home Detention Curfew Scheme. Surely, as this has already proved to have a 95 per cent success rate, it would follow that we should all be chipped, preventing all future crime. I mean, if you are a law-abiding citizen, you would surely have no qualms in helping to do your part in creating a safe, victimless environment?

Here's to 2020 – let us relax in the knowledge that advancement in this field will inevitably be the key to cracking down on crime for the good of society. After all, a crimeless environment must surely bring about freedom for one and all?

the vision-airy (U213517)

My Round (A861455)

by Emily Angle (U205316) ✪✪✪✪

It's 12:30, and the bar is just getting busy. It's my round and I dread the approach to the conveyor belt bar, where the snacks whizz past and adverts for post-inebriation services flash frantically on the screens.

You can get anything these days: someone to drive your car back to your house with you or without you; someone to phone your wife and tell her in your own completely sober voice that you'll be home in an hour; the sobering-up service offered by the NHS in an attempt to claw back some money from its rapidly dwindling budgets.

On my way to the bar, I spot a couple of girls putting coins into the vending machine for a packet of Phags – those little tubes of gases which have taken over from the old-fashioned carcinogenic alternatives – available in exhilarating nitrous oxide, refreshing oxygen and relaxing narcotic.

I join the throng to get served. The cameras above the bar sweep across the faces and a computer calculates the order of the queue. The staff all wear shiny earpieces, which tell them who to serve; any mistake and the earpiece emits a shrieking wail.

As I wait, I eye up the bar snacks: truffle scratchings, macrobiotic brown rice puffs in ready salted and miso flavour, and Stilton moments. I grab a bag of pancetta fries and a box of macadamia nuts as a chirpy woman arrives to take my order.

What I really hanker for is a traditional Cosmopolitan, but they're really only available for the old dears around Christmas. Instead, I order a half-litre of beer, a guarana and gingko biloba infused vodka, a hot sake, and two large glasses of Red. Red is foul, but it's way too late to start having standards. After the genetic experiments on the vineyards of France, California, Australia, New Zealand and South Africa, the only real wine fit to drink is

THE FOOD WILL BE IN TUBES AND VERY NOTORIOUS.

NICHOLAS L FLETCHER (U214391)

Bulgarian. Even so, I'd still prefer it to the synthetic wine even with its promise of a hangover-free morning.

I fork over a fifty and watch my order disappear down the conveyor belt where it will reappear at the corner table. I know there won't be any change, but if there were I would tip the beautifully regular 'waitress service' that the underground network of belts provides. Anything that means I don't have to lug a tray across the crowded room, spilling pounds' worth of booze with every jostle.

By the time I make it back to the table, the drinks have arrived, been drunk (apart from my cooling sake) and the next victim begins to make his way towards the bar.

In the year 2020 all food will fall under the European Directive Wind Act that states:

'All production of natural wind in the year 2020 is to cease in the interest of political correctness, social sensitivity and to maintain the stability of the ozone layer, particularly over the South Pole and parts of Bedfordshire.'

This will particularly apply to foods such as radishes, baked beans, eggs (especially when mashed with mayonnaise), Brussels sprouts, cabbage, curry (of all temperatures), pickled onions, hops (when used for real ale), Pot Noodles, mushy peas, cheese (especially when served with cauliflower), cauliflower (especially when served with cheese), broccoli, raisins, raw apples – all of which will have to be Genetically Modified Wind (GMW) compliant.

Dale Sergent (U216081)

I think that in the future all farm animals raised for meat will be obsolete. Meat will be grown in giant laboratories of cell cultures where cells will be reproduced endlessly without the threat of disease or the cruelty now deemed necessary.

Researcher 210602

The Rose & Crown (plc) (A998346)

by Steve Daniels (U220872)

I walked into the pub today
To buy a pound of sprouts,
And met the elderly vicar's wife
Gaily trotting out.

'I only went in for stamps,' she said
By way of apology.
'But then I stayed for a sherry –
Well, maybe two or three.'

Our village pub, that bastion
Of carefree inebriation,
Is now the village 'everything',
Thanks to diversification.

We used to be a sober bunch –
A fine, upstanding lot.
But now we're always in the pub,
Every one of us a sot.

Through the door marked 'Public Bar',
And past the nearly-new bazaar,
The automotive parts display,
The local meeting of AA,
I found the landlord in the rear.

'Ice cream? Videos? Turkish rugs?
Pile cream? Prescription drugs?
Groceries? A joint of meat?
Stereo? Reclining seat?
Or maybe just a beer?'

'I'll have a quick one, as you ask;
I'm meant to be grocery shopping.
I'll have a pint of Post Office Ale;
But mind, I won't be stopping.'

A commotion in the other bar
Then caused us some distress
As the local health and fitness champ
Had a cardiac arrest.

'It's Mr Jones, he's dead,' they said,
Now what are we to do?'
'Don't worry,' said the landlord,
'I'm the undertaker, too.'

And that's how life is nowadays
In villages in The Shires.
The pub is there for everything
To rent or buy or hire.

But somehow it's not quite the same;
Now it's part of the daily grind.
The pub was somewhere just to drink
And gradually unwind.

The clock was reading half past two
When I eventually staggered out.
And then I staggered in again –
I'd forgot the ruddy sprouts.

EU Directive 2,000,000,002 (A987591)

by Frances Green (U220930) ✪✪✪✪

Hereby giving effect to sub-clauses of the
following existing statutory instruments:

Global Species Equal Rights Agreement (2018)
Genus Transplantation Equality Laws (2010)
(2015) (2019)
Quadruped-Bipedal Equivalent Working
Regulations (2017)
Higher Animals Equal Pay Agreement (2017)
(Amended 2019)
Flexible Working (Time Off for Calving and
Lambing) Act (2012)
Artificial Insemination Bovine Parent Tracing
Agency Act (2015)
Quadruped Contractor – Non-intellectual Property
Rights Law (2009)

1 It is hereby noted and seriously meant
That milk provision now requires signed ethical
    consent.

2 The rights of each and every cow, respected and
    deserved,
Are by this statutory act legitimately served.

3 Each bovine representative empowered by legal
    moves
Must authorise each milking by a signing of the
    hooves.

4 From now on farmers break the law unless a
    contract's signed
With each cow every morning to confirm she

doesn't mind
The physical extraction, and understands that she
Can take her fees from income that's divided
    equally.

5 Clause 2 in Bovine Contracts governs subse-
    quent milk use.
Cows now have rights to mandate sale for butter-
    scotch or mousse.

6 And any profits hereby made must now by law
    be halved
With shares for her descendants once she's done
    her bit and calved.

7 Core rates for milk can't deviate from European
    norms
Unless both parties so agree and fill in opt-out
    forms.
(Transgenic milk expressed in bags for inter-
    stellar flights
Is one such case where both might bid for extra
    bonus rights.)

8 Of course, the EU understands the burden of
    this change
And will resource more access to its special legal
    range.

9 Do seek advice, but in so doing, please just bear
    in mind
Such laws promote the betterment of life for
    species-kind.

Around the World in 80 Minutes (A935020)

by Faizy25 (U214802) ✪✪✪✪✪

I thought that travel was supposed to be fun, but I find myself dreading my next trip. Ever since the budget airlines were able to reduce costs and combine this with the latest technologies to take us to far-off destinations, I seem to be in a different part of the world every weekend. Flights that used to take several hours now only take a fraction of that time.

It is Friday afternoon and I am still getting over the cold I picked up from last weekend's trip to Japan. I am not in a good mood. My body does not know in which time zone it is operating and I desperately need some sleep.

The phone has not rung yet, meaning that my wife has been unable to book a last-minute flight. With a bit of luck a weekend in front of the television watching the 2020 Cup Final beckons.

But just as I pack my things to rush out of the office, I get the dreaded call.

'Hello, darling,' she says. 'Guess what? We're off to Mexico for the weekend. I found such a great bargain on GoeasyJet.com. I was just surfing the Internet on my watch and the offer popped up

out of the blue. A weekend in the sun and exploring ancient mystical ruins for only £50! They say that if the journey takes more than an hour we get our money back.'

'Fantastic!' I lie. 'I can't wait to get out there.'

Six hours later I find myself struggling up the steps of an ancient temple in the jungle. The heat and humidity are unbearable. My watch suddenly makes a bleeping sound and the instant replay function is activated – United have just gone ahead.

'How can you think about football in a place like this?' she sighs.

On the beach I take out my digital planner and catch up with some work. My wife looks at me disapprovingly. If we stay in one place for the next few hours, there is a slim chance that I will meet the deadline my boss set me.

'You're so boring sometimes. You should be relaxing, not working.'

I sneeze again. My cold has returned.

'Don't worry. The heat will do wonders for your cold. In fact, I was thinking that a trip to Australia would be a nice idea for next Saturday. How about it?'

Drug Legalisation (A918704)

by Therion Ware (U210356) ✪✪✪✪

Martin Lees Legalisation: The Consequences (THC Publishing 2020, London) is the first comprehensive review of the wider consequences of the complete legalisation of drugs in the EU in 2017, and as such it is a timely and controversial volume.

As is now well known, the 'Addiction Vaccination' (ADV) of every EU child at six months guarantees that there will be no 'next generation' of addicts, and it was on the back of this major advance that full legalisation was enabled. The next generation will be able to take or leave recreational drugs (RDs) on their merits, with no element of psychological or physiological compulsion.

Where Lees wholly strikes home is in his forthright examination of the ADV issue. ADV simply doesn't 'take' on post-pubescent individuals (progress towards a version that does remains frustratingly slow) and nothing is expected before 2030 at the earliest. How then could government justify legalisation when the overwhelming majority of addicts are adults? Was it irresponsibility of the first order to base such a massive change in social policy on an advance that may never come to fruition?

Lees thinks not, arguing that the reduction in crimes against property

the reduction in crimes against property and persons more than justifies legalisation

and persons (down by 93 per cent since 2017) more than justifies legalisation, and while it is difficult to canvas the opinion of those who have not been mugged or burgled, the public broadly appears to approve. True, the number of addicts has increased, but the availability of good quality regulated doses of the drug of choice from government 'up licences', as well as substantive advice on 'mix and match' drug use, has resulted in a significant decrease percentage-wise in addict mortality.

Paradoxically, the personal freedom bestowed by legalisation has been paid for with the loss of other freedoms. It is now illegal to drive under the influence of any

heavy purchasers being refused public liability insurance, jobs and adoption rights

amount of any RD (including alcohol); personal liability for loss or injury to another whilst under the influence of any RD, including alcohol, is unlimited, with substantial terms of imprisonment mandatory for those who harm another whilst under the influence of RDs.

However, it is the 'list' that causes most concern.

Purchase of RDs requires age and identity verification by retinal ID, and the list of purchasers is freely available from the EU social contract website. It has been of significant interest to insurance companies, heavy purchasers being refused public liability insurance, jobs and, in several instances, adoption rights.

We are no longer destined to live on the ground. Multi-tiered cities now float high in the sky. Transport takes only one form: the personal vehicle, which can take us anywhere we like, as fast as we like and we don't even need to learn how to operate it.

With Gravity Manipulation, land-territory is no longer a contentious issue, as there's plenty of space for everyone.

Huw Langridge (TU212096)

Film of the Year: *9/11* (A922547)

by Phil Colvin (U207971) ✪✪✪✪

2020 will see the premiere of *9/11*, the definitive Hollywood interpretation of the most audacious terrorist act of all time seen through the eyes of two star-crossed lovers.

Advertised as a historical spectacle, *9/11* will receive tremendous pre-release hype for its ground-breaking special effects, including the most risky stunt ever committed to celluloid. For the makers, it will be a triumphant return to the epic historical disasters of the 90s, *Titanic*, *Saving Private Ryan* and *Pearl Harbor*, and to the days when elaborate stunt sequences were performed for real instead of through computers. 'The attack itself,' the producer points out, 'would have been terrifyingly real for anyone in those towers. This isn't about entertainment. It's our responsibility as historians to present this incident as accurately as possible. It's something we've forgotten in these days of computer effects-laden films.'

9/11 could go on to storm the 2021 Oscars

The project has been greeted with scepticism from critics, many of whom comment that they are watching little more than a two-hour fictional love story of stunning banality set against the background of incredible pyrotechnics. However, *9/11* will surpass all expectations and go on to be one of the greatest box office successes of all time. Audiences will flock back time and again to witness two of Hollywood's hottest young talents be torn apart by the heart-breaking effects of the disaster.

'Their love story,' a tabloid critic points out, 'provides an emotional centre for the film. It gives the audience something human to grasp between the fire and brimstone and reminds us that, in the face of tragedy, love conquers all.'

Despite persistent condemnation from the September 11th Foundation for its trivialising of both human tragedy and the historical context of the event, *9/11* could go on to storm the 2021 Oscars. Rumours abound of a special 'Services to History' award presented by filmmaker James Cameron.

Celebrating 58 years at the cinema, Bond is back in his 40th explosive adventure.

In this latest instalment, Bond (Sean Clonery) is enlisted to save the mining colony on Pluto from the evil clutches of SPECTRE.

In their effort to retain the retro aspect of Bond, the writers combined two of the best-known Bond baddies: 'Blofeld' and 'Oddjob'. 'Baron Oddfeld' is played by notorious cyber-gangster rapper Fir Q and portrays a far superior baddy to the most recent 'Dr Negative' played by prototype humanoid 'G74'.

Johanthan Ross Jnr. (U214770)

After the shock that 2016's summer blockbuster, 'Jolt', was shot entirely with no actual film footage of humans in it, the use of digital stand-ins has become common-place. Films are re-shot using digital actors, endings can be re-worked in the edit suite with no re-filming costs and no one fights the 'Big Four' film companies for pay rises. Most are too scared to lose what little work they do get thrown.

But perhaps the most frightening part is of Tom Cruise, who licenses out his 'full bodily image' for six or seven Made-for-Digital-Download (MfDD) films each year, despite not having been seen in public for some time. While this may be good for Tom, many true film fans are beginning to question why they are shelling out so much to download what in reality is an unplayable computer game.

BadInfluence (U214197)

The Science of Fair Play (A867062)

by Dr Bernard Dixon (U208322)

Just as today's weight-lifters and boxers are restricted to competing with opponents of similar build, by 2020 athletes in many other sports may have to be categorised according to their genes. We can already identify and locate individual genes within the chromosomes. Genes that influence physical attributes relevant to sporting prowess are beginning to emerge.

One striking example came to light when Finnish investigators studied a group of closely related families whose members had distinctive ruddy faces. All of these individuals carried a gene that caused them to produce greater quantities of the hormone erythropoietin (EPO) than normal. This, in turn, caused abnormally high levels of red blood cells in their bloodstream. Their blood carries more oxygen to their muscles, enabling them to move faster and more efficiently without their hearts pumping any more blood. It was no surprise that one family member had won an Olympic medal for cross-country skiing.

The misuse of EPO to achieve track and field success has become a major issue in recent years. Although its primary applications are medical – for example, reducing the number of blood transfusions

> **by 2020 athletes may have to be categorised according to their genes**

required by patients on regular kidney dialysis – the hormone is also open to abuse. EPO has thus been added to the list of substances banned in competitive sport. Yet no blame whatsoever can be attached to someone who has a high natural level of this hormone in his or her bloodstream. Its source is 'in the genes'.

Another gene of this sort, reported in *Nature* in 1998, is involved in the regulation of blood pressure. A study of mountaineers showed that one version of the gene was associated with elite performance in high-altitude mountain climbing. Repetitive weight-lifting skills following training were also far superior in individuals with the gene than in those lacking it. Again, this constitutes a clear, measurable difference in aptitude between one person and another.

Back in the 1960s, screening designed to ensure that only individuals with the female complement of sex chromosomes were permitted to take part in women's competitions was deemed mandatory. The procedure has often been questioned. Now, more rigorous genetic testing may take its place to ensure fair competition in sport.

Scottish Football (A979626)
by Tommy Mac (U216022) ✪✪✪✪

Without fear of contradiction I can predict the following Scottish football events for the year 2020:

Celtic or Rangers will win the Scottish Premier Championship League. Rangers or Celtic will win the Scottish FA Cup. Celtic or Rangers will win the Scottish League Cup. Celtic AND Rangers will both qualify for the European Champions league. They will not get past the qualifying stages, so will go into the UEFA Cup. They will both win their qualifying games, then lose.

Neither of them will manage to get past the Christmas break, and the following year it will begin all over again, with exactly the same outcome.

FIFA World Cup 2018 (A935985)

by Tony Digba (U213534)

Nigeria 2018

The twenty-first FIFA World Cup was hosted by the Nigerians with all the fanfare and aplomb that the Africans seem to make their own. There were plenty of goals, controversy and surprises. This year will always be remembered as the year of the Spaniards, as Spain romped its way to victory. Even the massive home support of the Nigerians for their team in the finals could not stop the swagger and cutting edge of Spain. We may yet have to wait another four years to see an African team's hands on the cup!

After suffering decades of being called perennial underachievers, the Spanish were not to be denied their moment of glory. The final match between Nigeria and Spain would go down in history as one of the classics. Spain, who were 1-0 down within the first 10 minutes, fought back gallantly with a brace scored by their top striker, Nigerian-born Ade Ola. Ola called his winning goal a bittersweet moment. The future is indeed orange...

New FIFA rules paved the way for the advent of the super-athlete. The previous year saw a controversial rule, lifting the ban on new performance-enhancing drugs. Sports authorities had bent to pressure by drug companies who had proved that these were no longer harmful to anyone. A FIFA spokesman stated, 'They are safe and everyone is taking them anyway!'

Germany, for the first time ever, failed to progress beyond the first round after being beaten 1-0 by England in an epic contest. Veteran England striker Wayne Rooney scored the decisive goal. Holland, the

Germany, for the first time ever, failed to progress beyond the first round after being beaten by England (1-0)

pre-tournament favourites, also failed to progress. After a 3-0 opening loss to the host country Nigeria, they never got back into their stride, losing all subsequent matches.

The surprise team of the tournament was Costa Rica, going all the way to the last four only to be beaten by the brilliant Spanish in the semi-finals. The other semi-final was a mouth-watering encounter between host nation Nigeria and England. The Nigerians made an amazing comeback from 3-1 to draw 3-3 in extra-time. Nigeria won the game on penalties 5-4, with the decisive penalty miss by England's captain.

Green and Easy (A985502)

by Michael Meacher MP (U221058) ✪✪✪✪

save the planet

A vision of a green future? Easy! Our future must be one in which we live in harmony with the natural world, respecting the limits of our planet to absorb pollution and provide resources for human consumption. Human beings, like all other species, depend on habitable ecosystems to survive. We need to change the way that our society and our economies operate.

Why? First, because we should respect and preserve the beauty and astonishing diversity of our natural world. But also

> **can we reconcile environmental concerns with our desire for a fairer society?**

because it is in our own interest, and in the interest of future generations. Pollution, traffic and green spaces are issues that affect the quality of our lives here and now. And biodiversity (the richness and variety of species on our planet) is important for our long-term futures.

Our impact on the environment is deeply interwoven with our social and economic activities. Can we reconcile environmental concerns with our desire for a fairer society and for economic development? Can we have our cake and eat it? Well actually, yes we can! We do not need to reduce our quality of life. But we do need to make major changes in the way our economies and societies treat our environment, so that we respect the constraints of our fragile planet.

Climate change is perhaps the greatest environmental challenge of all. Global warming is already with us. Temperatures are projected to rise by up to 5.8°C this century – ten times the current increase of 0.6°C in the last century. The number of people affected by floods globally has risen from seven million people in the 1960s to 150 million now. In 1998 two-thirds of Bangladesh was under water for months on end, affecting 30 million people. In the UK, the figures are much lower, but severe enough. The Environment Agency believes that

five million people and 185,000 businesses are at risk of flooding in the future in this country.

Energy and transport are the primary sources of the emissions that cause global warming. By 2050, international scientific experts believe that we need to reduce these emissions by 60 per cent to tackle climate change. The UK and other nations will have to adapt quickly to tackle this. The UK Government recently published a new energy strategy that included the aim of reducing emissions of carbon dioxide (the most important contributor to global warming) by some 60 per cent from current levels by about 2050. And a low-carbon economy is not only good for the environment, investment in energy efficiency is stimulating employment across the country.

My vision for the future is that we achieve this kind of change, adapting our society to respect environmental limits, while continuing to achieve economic development and tackling social issues. It is in all our interests to make that vision a reality.

2020: A Space Odyssey or Just Another Year? (A922259)

by B. James Proctor (U213463) ✪✪✪✪

The year 2020 seems a long way off, doesn't it? But it's only 17 years. Can we really be so ignorant as to think that in 17 years we'll be living in a Utopian society? If we consider how long it has taken us to get this far technologically, it will be a long and winding road until a human can call a spaceship home. So, therefore, we must consider the possibilities:

Earth

Another planet

As you see, the latter will not be achievable in 17 years, no matter what happens. With Earth's resources declining at an alarming rate, we must think about conserving our planet before it becomes our deathbed. There are many perils humans face in the not so distant future: over-population, pollution, global warming, a nuclear or a biological war. All of these problems are human-created ones. If we are to colonise other planets, hadn't we better make sure that we humans will be around in order to do so?

Without Earth we cannot survive, therefore it stands to reason that we should attempt to keep our planet tidy in order to live. But why should we bother to do so in this money-oriented world, where our only thought is where the next dollar is coming from? Humans have turned into scrooges.

if we are to colonise other planets, hadn't we better make sure humans will be around in order to do so

We must consider everything we do and place it in relevance to our species' continued survival and its co-habitation with all the other life of our planet. It is possible that we have already developed a hydrogen engine and that it is being kept hidden under patent laws by the heads of petrol companies not wanting to lose profit. I feel that, if we do not curb our selfish ways, we will be in a dire situation in years to come.

I'd end the starvation of every nation
And people would cry from love's elation
Tara Palmer-Tomkinson (U219157)

All Human Life Is on TV (A962462)

by Thomas Sutcliffe (U218785) ✪✪✪✪

'Human kind cannot bear very much reality,' wrote T. S. Eliot. But apparently there's absolutely no limit to the amount of reality television they can take in. So is this a momentary blip in cultural fashion – a prurient version of tulip mania – or does it represent a more permanent change in the way we tell stories about ourselves? There certainly isn't a shortage of people willing to declare the genre dead or to cackle over fading audience figures for some specific example of the current taste for voyeurism. But a funeral service would be premature for the following reasons.

Firstly, improvements in broadcasting technology have, in almost every case, led to a greater representation of ordinary people's lives in the media. When sound recordings could not be edited, the voice of real people was usually scripted by professional broadcasters. The arrival of tape recorders allowed them to speak

> **reality programming isn't reaching the end of its life... it is just beginning**

naturally for themselves for the first time.

A similar revolution was brought about by lightweight video cameras – a technology, which entirely changed the rules as far as television was concerned. The vivid immediacy of video-diaries led to soap docs, which, in turn, led to the current breed of reality game show and a new type of drama, which aped the naturalism of documentaries. The arrival of new ways of picturing ordinary lives – such as video-telephones and photo messaging – will soon be absorbed into television programmes and is likely to change the rules still further.

Secondly, narrative culture has always had prurience at its heart. Stories depend on our desire to know how other people live and love and cope with problems that we might encounter ourselves – and technology now means that real lives can supply the raw material for such rehearsals. There is a moral question here – about what happens when genuine dilemmas and distress become public entertainment. But the moral advantage is nowhere near as clear-cut as some critics of reality television like to make out.

Is it better for the entire nation to be preoccupied by the fantastical machinations of Dallas oil millionaires or by the attempts of real people to get on with each other in close confinement? As social animals,

understanding how other people feel and think is genetically embedded in us as a priority. It will not be erased simply because some television programmes are cruel and distasteful.

Besides, reality programming is not reaching the end of its life. It is just beginning it. And there are already signs of growing maturity to the form, as producers realise that empathy and concerned curiosity can be just as powerful as mockery.

Two predictions are safe in this field. Media companies will deliver programmes and formats that currently sit safely within the confines of satirical invention (who would have believed *Big Brother* 15 years ago?) and audiences will continue to be gripped by them. It may be a failing to become so engrossed by the experiences of others, but without it we wouldn't actually be human.

This Christmas, brace yourselves for the arrival of Santa Claus Academy 2020! Twelve bearded men will enter the £12m mansion, built at the North Pole to commemorate Queen Elizabeth's Diamond Jubilee and the colonisation of the Arctic (or New Milton Keynes as it is now officially recognised), to fight for the title of Santa Claus... The twelve men will be taught to use the 'scramjet' technology on Santa's newly commissioned plane, 'Reindeer 8', which will allow them to reach the necessary speed to deliver presents to every child in the world in one night. Other lessons include, 'How To Shake Your Belly Like A Bowl Full Of Jelly', 'Mince Pie and Whisky Appreciation' and 'Beard Maintenance'.

Neil Ridulfa (U214824)

Complications Arise for New Baby Show (A872354)

by Jimster [h2g2 Editorial] (U292)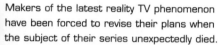

Makers of the latest reality TV phenomenon have been forced to revise their plans when the subject of their series unexpectedly died.

Life Before Birth was planned as a 24/7 look at the life of an embryo from the three-month mark through to birth. The mother's womb was fitted with minute cameras, which enabled viewers to see the unborn baby via the live website and in the edited highlights broadcast each evening.

But after the mother (who cannot be named for legal reasons) tragically miscarried, the producers were afraid their project would be brought to an end.

That was, until someone came up with the bright idea of expanding the project. In the forthcoming *Born Famous*, 12 mothers will be fitted with the womb-cam system and, as the weeks go by, viewers will be able to vote for which of the babies they wish to see born on the live 'Delivery Night' six months later.

Unlike other reality shows, which rely on the traditional formula of regular evictions from the game, each mother will be in the project until the very end. 'We felt that the sense of rejection and loss might be too emotionally unbalancing for the mother and, therefore, might pose a danger to the embryo,' said a spokesperson for the show yesterday.

This is despite the fact that an audition-style show will have already rejected an estimated 1,500 expectant mothers by the time the final 12 reach the screen.

Predictably, there have been some complaints regarding the show's taste and decency and concerns over its exploitative nature, but these have been dismissed by the show's producers. 'There has never been anything like this level of interactivity with a pre-birth before. Now we will be able to see for the first time the effects that the outside world have upon an unborn child. We will be able to see their reactions to music, or whether or not they recognise or react to voices.'

With the ever-increasing popularity of reality TV programming, it is now estimated that 72 per cent of the population are considered celebrities. The demand for information on these 'celebrities' has made newspaper sales soar. There has been an estimated 150 new newspapers launched to keep up with the demand.

Bamboozled (U216718)

E.T. (A912944)

by AngelEyes (U210402) ✪✪✪✪

At 18:20 GMT, on 23 February 2020, a signal was received by a communications satellite in Earth's orbit. The transmission was sent from a small robot spacecraft on the surface of Jupiter's icy moon, Europa, and it heralded the greatest discovery in the history of humankind. Below the freezing surface of Europa, nearly 500m miles away from Earth, life had been discovered. The ocean beneath the ice, warmed by geothermal activity from the moon's core and kept moving by Jupiter's extreme gravity, was rife with microbial activity. These organisms, while not being 'little green men', were similar to primitive microbes found on Earth and gave conclusive proof that life is not unique.

the discovery brought people together in the way religion always advocated

Within minutes the news had spread to almost every corner of our planet and, even though at one stage it looked like society might break down trying to comprehend the enormity of it all, people seemed to accept the news with maturity and intelligence. Indeed, the ramifications of the discovery were such that global society improved considerably in the days and weeks following. Crime rates fell, strangers spoke to each other in the streets and it seemed as though the whole planet was smiling. Ironically, while doing more to disprove the existence of God than anything else in history, the discovery had brought people together in the way that religion had always advocated.

That was until 15 April when a fundamental religious group, having decided that a world which renounced God did not deserve the gift of life, orchestrated a planet-wide release of a genetically modified Ebola

society might break down trying to comprehend the enormity of it all

virus. The virus claimed the last human lives before the year was out.

In space, man's influence is still felt. Pioneer 10, launched in March 1972 and powered by radioisotope generators, sits in the freezing blackness of space. The gold plate it carries, etched with greetings from man, still survives to carry the message of the race that created it.

In the year 2020, scientists will realise that spiders are actually an alien life form that drifted in egg form through space and landed on Earth one million years ago.

The inhabitants of Earth are genetically programmed to naturally recognise native life forms and when they see spiders they subconsciously recognise them as aliens.

Which is why so many people are inexplicably frightened of spiders...

Peta (U24)

Harry Potter and the Mortgage Repayments of Doom (A959989)

by Mark R Edwards (U217481) ★★★★

After completing the seventh Harry Potter book J. K. Rowling, the world's richest woman, bowed to intense pressure from adults pining for their childhood and started a second series.

This is the blurb from the fifth instalment of this series, *Harry Potter and the Mortgage Repayments of Doom*, the follow-up to the acclaimed *Harry Potter and the Kidney Stone*.

'Kids today,' grumbles Harry, 'aren't interested in magic'

It's the summer holidays and soon Harry Potter, the most famous wizard in the world, will be starting his fifth year as a teacher at Hogwarts School of Witchcraft and Wizardry. But all is not well in the Potter household and the wider wizarding world. Admissions at Hogwarts are at an all-time low. 'Kids today,' grumbles Harry, 'aren't interested in magic. All they care about is watching *Clone Idol* and downloading footage of World War III to watch on their newfangled nano-phones.'

Harry's account at Gringotts has long since run dry and he is behind on his mortgage payments. To make matters worse, his wife – the Muggle-born Sarah who Harry met in *Harry Potter and the Shotgun Wedding* – is not happy. She wants to know why Harry is not more like his cousin, Dudley Dursley MP. Ron and Hermione have just had their first child

if that wasn't enough, Harry is also having problems with his prostate

and have little time for Harry and his woes.

Then Harry discovers a terrible plot. Draco Malfoy wants to get rid of Harry and sell Hogwarts to Disney so they can turn it into a theme park. And as if that wasn't enough, Harry is also having problems with his prostate.

Can Harry ward off the Bailiff Trolls, get the nation's kids interested in sorcery again and keep his wife happy? Will he be able to defeat Malfoy and Mickey Mouse? Will the antibiotics work? Find out in this witty, parodic and ever-so-slightly-depressing novel for adults and the few children who are still interested in such things.

Further developments in combating the debilitative effects of ageing on human tissue have had the result of greatly increasing the career length of top sportsmen.

This has been particularly notable in individual sports where 25-time Wimbledon Champion, Wayne Clapham of Australia, recently completed the Grand Slam for a record 14th time. Whilst his achievements are amazing, they are not unprecedented, as this year, Tiger Woods completed the golfing Grand Slam for the 57th time.

Dave Klein (U214606)

The new demographic cool group are the 'Wrinklies' — the seventy-somethings who have managed to escape from 50 years of debt misery and the shackles of style.

John Butcher (U213635)

Anarchy in the UK (A930593)

by Banalitycrow (U214773)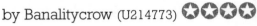

It was announced today that Britons are amongst the richest people in Europe. The findings were made by the Department For The Wastage Of Taxpayers' Money That Hasn't Been Used On Politicians' Pay Rises. This all stems, of course, from the government's decision to adopt the euro in 2008. At the time there were 137 euros to the pound. The exchange rate, when the conversion went through, made some people become millionaires overnight.

Scientists are also celebrating the creation of the first genetically modified politician.

rumours that London will drown within 3 years appear to be unfounded

It has a 'self destruct' gene that activates when they break an election promise. Critics deem it as 'too little too late'.

Rumours that London will be drowned by the English Channel in the next three years appear to be unfounded.

Northerners are said to be 'devastated' by the news. Contingency plans to put the capital on specially designed stilts have been sidelined until the danger is more imminent. When asked how imminent the danger has to be, a British office spokesperson said, 'Oh, two or three days before, I should think.'

The Thames Barrier, given an artificial intelligence last year, is said to be 'unamused' and was considering relocating to the Bannoch Burn where it can at least listen to Boy George in peace.

The GM crops problem reached a peak yesterday when an entire field of turnips walked to the British Office and demanded equal rights for veg. A flustered British Office Unit said, 'I'm sorry, but we can't talk to veg,' which gained him an instant discrimination charge from the mobile court. In a related incident, a field of cabbages are campaigning for the use of their name in reference to drunk or stupid people to be outlawed on racist grounds.

These cases could set a precedent for Brussels sprouts currently campaigning in Belgium for the right to stand for European Parliament. But then, who'd notice if they did get in?

As England is not a safe place to live anymore, due to terrorism and badly resourced public services, Wales is a magnet for families unable to live in England. Houses in London now fetch up to 4m euros and people are unable to secure a stable home.

Welsh Premier Dafydd Morgan said that he and his government were seriously considering action against the English Government for its failure to control its economy and inability to stop immigration.

Researcher U218512

STATE OF THE NATION (A896556)

BY LOU (U210384) ✪✪✪✪

Following the 2010 riot by architects and interior designers, who were desperate for something to design, the Green Belt was abolished and the cityscape took over. England is now one huge metropolis, called 'London' by its inhabitants and 'a mess' by the long-disbanded EU.

Now there is no housing shortage; in fact there's a surplus, with couples being encouraged to live apart and buy their children homes from the age of six. Following the eventual swap to the euro, England's economy plummeted as people madly tried to calculate costs in 'old money'. More riots ensued, again mostly initiated by the interior designers (no one knew how to use the money, let alone wanted to give it to Lawrence Llewelyn-Bowen). Soon London was back to the faithful pound and the interior design business boomed.

The third term in office of the Monster Raving Loony Party resulted in insane laws like having to drive backwards on a Sunday, but they abolished equally stupid rules such as the so-called 'London Congestion Charge', which is now seen as another folly of the olden days.

Due to this, and many other slightly insane laws, London has now been launched into the centre of the Atlantic by Europe. Huge fans, one in New York and one in Madrid, keep the island at bay somewhere in the middle of the ocean. Wales, Scotland and Ireland, however, spontaneously broke away from London and are now happily living somewhere south of Hawaii.

'Local' Food For Real Communities (A982208)

by Zac Goldsmith (U220689) ✪✪✪✪

Twice in a fortnight Britain's collective heart stopped cold. No sooner had people recovered from the news that a nuclear power plant had come within minutes of meltdown, following a mistake by a sleepy worker, than a terrorist had attempted to fly a small plane into the ancillary coolant buildings at Sellafield. Twice in a fortnight Britain faced being rendered virtually uninhabitable. But it had sparked the end of nuclear power and, with continuing complications in oil-producing nations, it had helped trigger the beginning of an era of clean, decentralised and renewable energy.

In many ways, 2023 was a good time to be British. That is not to say it was a Utopia. Certainly the recent building spree on what remained of Britain's green-field sites had taken its toll. Villages that for centuries had been distinct, had merged haphazardly into a clumsy sprawl. And because new developments were built on the assumption of the motorcar, they were more commuter zones than communities, and lacked the usual characteristics of an organic settlement. It had been decided that, with their cars, inhabitants would find all they needed in the distant hyper-markets. So there had been no provision for shops, post offices or markets. Now they had become human dustbins where people aspired to one thing – leaving as soon as they possibly could.

But even here, there were signs of recovery. The rapid move some ten years earlier towards a localised food system had effectively marginalised the hypermarkets. They hadn't been designed with local production and distribution in mind, and their vast centralised structures just couldn't adapt. All but a handful of smaller operations were abandoned, their roles being taken up by a massive resurgence of farmers' and co-operative markets. In most communities the transition was smooth and welcome. In the commuter zones, it was less so. But necessity, they say, is the mother of invention and with the hyper-markets closing, they soon adapted. Some had even taken on the appearance of real, functioning communities.

Elsewhere, the countryside was flourishing and, for the first time in decades, there was

villages merged haphazardly into a clumsy sprawl

an unexpected return by urbanites to rural Britain. For nearly a century successive governments had pursued agricultural policy that was globally oriented. The very notion that a country should be equipped to provide for its own basic food needs had been regarded by decision-makers as defunct, if not ludicrous. The assumption had been that the global food

FOLLOWING THE FAILURE TO BAN HUNTING FOXES CONTINUE TO ADAPT TO URBAN LIVING

system would last forever, that an advanced nation would always be able to depend on the volatile commodity markets for its survival. But a series of scares, not least the ceaseless oil wars and resulting international turmoil, had left people with a feeling of vulnerability. And, with an increasingly unpredictable climate, countries had learned that their only hope was to do away with the vast industrial mono-cultures that had characterised agriculture for so long, and replace them with diverse, localised food systems that could withstand sudden alterations to the seasons.

Britain had set about regenerating a human-scale food economy, and the effect on the countryside was immediate. There being only so much grain or milk a community could absorb, local market pressures soon forced farmers to diversify their production. Away went the miles upon miles of single crops. In came the hedgerows that harboured the birds which removed the pestilent insects. And as farms were transformed, the chemical props that maintained artificial food systems became defunct. The countryside was gradually becoming something of a paradise.

In the year 2020 it will still be raining here in Britain.
Researcher 213580

Elvis Lives (A993693)

by Grease Weekly (U221277) ✪✪✪✪

Statistics have proved that eventually every fifth person in the world will be an Elvis impersonator. This thought must fill the soul of a real fan with the kind of icy cold, gut-wrenching, bum-puckering dread that makes grown men urinate in their own underwear.

Why? Because there has only ever been one decent attempt at impersonating the leather-clad, sexual rebel with the suggestive hips, and that was by the fat bloke in the

to a true fan an impersonator is a malformed caricature of what was once sacred

white jumpsuits that used to live in Memphis. No, to a true fan an impersonator is just a hideous malformed caricature of all that was once sacred. At the 'We-miss-him-so-much-we-still-wear-our-sideburns-like-him Women's Adoration Society', baldies with pretensions don't cut no ice – however many lip curls they do.

Just imagine it: you've booked an impersonator to entertain family and friends at Granny's funeral. In walks Huw Evans from Aberystwyth and bursts into his rendition of 'I wish I was in the land of cotton, old times there are not forgotten, look you, look you, look you… boyo'. Disaster! But it can be avoided.

Available now from Stars R Us®, The Personal Clonic Regeneration Unit (Pat. Pending) can turn any party into a success. Cleverly removed and preserved in a solution of peanut butter and bacon fat, the King's stray hairs now render unto us the DNA strands necessary to produce carbon copies of the porky lounge singer for your own personal enjoyment.

Yes, just pop a strand into your own machine, add water and switch on. A mere 12 hours later there'll be a little less conversation and a little more action at your happening party.

Anniversaries, karaoke parties – hands down, your knees-up will be the talk of the town. Not an Elvis fan? Don't worry! Here at Stars R Us® we have a huge collection of celebrity DNA. Just want to

Forties crooning more your style? Then load up your regeneration unit and get your very own Bing!

chill out, spark up a spliff and listen to some mellow reggae? Then whip up a Bob Marley. Bit of Forties crooning more your style? Then load up your regeneration unit, and when the bell goes ding, get your very own Bing!

Order your unit now and we'll throw in your first three celebs free!

The Stars R Us® Company nor any of its representatives can be held liable for disposal of carbon copy celebrities in any way.

The poor old dog has been frozen in the cryogenic chamber at the vets since early December because they are not allowed to clone a dead creature during the Christmas holidays. (After all, a clone is for life, not just for Christmas.)

They started the cloning process early in the new year. Finally today, my family and I have taken home the frozen old dog and had a first peek at our resurrected pet, Rosie 2.

Richard Thomas (U214618)

The Key to the Future (A931844)

by Richard Fair (U214623) ✪✪✪✪

I'm cold. So very, very cold.

Every bone and every joint is stiff and painful. I want to move about to get warm but my muscles are hard and heavy like lead. I can feel my heart straining to pump my blood through grudging veins.

Sleepless nights never used to bother me. Eventually, tiredness would catch up with me and I'd sleep heavily and soundly. But the feeling of waking up from a good night's sleep is just a distant memory now, because for me every night is a sleepless night.

It's just after 4 a.m. and I'm trying not to think about the cold and the debilitating fatigue of six months without sleep. The doctors say that the best therapy is to write down on paper my feelings and thoughts.

The most vivid are the most recent ones and they tend to revolve around ways to get myself warm or counter the tiredness. But the thoughts that disturb me are those that I realise are memories of people, places and experiences I must have known. But I have no real sense of them ever happening and there is no emotion attached to them. They are just there. They seem a whole life apart. And I suppose, in a way, they are.

The only thing I do know for sure is that, at the time, I didn't want to die. I wanted to live forever and I thought that having my body frozen would help me escape the one thing I feared most.

So, I was sold cryogenics as the key to my future: a way to live again, a way to cheat Death. But Death has no time for charlatans. So I spend night after night trying as many ways as I can to end this living Hell, knowing full well that Death wants nothing more to do with me.

Don't Blame It on the Sunshine (A987672)

by Gemma Sutton (U215101) ✪✪✪

15 August 2020

Today, a surprised George W. Bush scrambled up onto a large podium in New York. As remarkable as it may seem, he was not receiving an award for outstanding achievement. He was merely trying to escape the rising water around him.

After years of disregarding the advice and research of top scientists from around the world, Bush can no longer ignore the issue of global warming, as his wet socks are likely to be a more or less constant reminder!

Breaking news

Reports are just in that Bush has got carried away, but not with his policies this time. He has been swept away by the sea. Mother Nature will have her revenge.

It's mid-January 2020. I remember back in 2003, I wondered what the future might be like... At first, I thought a way of understanding the levels of change possible was to look into the past. It being 2003, this took me back to 1986. I was ten years old and blissfully unaware of how Luke and Matt Goss were going to affect my entrance into the dreaded early teens. White shirt and red braces, anyone? The responsibilities of life had never crossed my mind. Neither had their comeback in 2015.

James Foley (U214386)

Rubber Ducks (A923537)

by Caper Plip (U180841)

Following the tragic death of a child whilst in the bathtub, a British Safety Standards spokesperson has announced that the rubber duck, indigenous to the bathroom, will no longer be allowed in its native habitat as of this year.

This shock revelation comes after the death of a three-year-old boy from Portsmouth, who cannot be named for legal reasons. He was having a bath in his own home when his five-year-old brother encouraged him to swallow the rubber duck for a bet. The duck got wedged in the boy's throat and he died soon after from asphyxiation. The duck in question measured 12 cm (4¹/₂ in), conformed to all safety standards and has since been destroyed.

The age range for warnings on toys with small parts was raised from 18 months to 36 months in 2010 after a similar occurrence with a two-year-old girl and a pair of fluffy dice. Now British Safety Standards believe that the banning of all products under 46 cm (1¹/₂ ft) from the bathroom ensures security for people of all ages. Those products formerly allowed in the bathroom will either be labelled 'Do not use in the bathtub', or to a more lenient extent, 'Do not place near water', with the usual warning advising against giving the product to children under 36 months. After the Pimlico Incident

the rubber duck will no longer be allowed in its native habitat

of 2013, when a 34-year-old intoxicated woman was found to have a selection of bathroom products lodged in her stomach, it was thought that more precautions were required to prevent such things occurring again.

Though the standard rubber duck may have become extinct, a company based in Cornwall has recently patented designs for a breed of 120 cm (4 ft) tall inflatable rubber ducks. As it is over the new limit of 46 cm (1¹/₂ ft), this has been deemed acceptable for bathtime use by people of all ages and is guaranteed by its creator to give just as much pleasure as the traditional duck, if not more.

The Wisdom of Children (A973550)

by Ute Navidi (U219838) ✪✪✪✪

Fatima rubs her eyes. It's ten o'clock and she needs to be online in an hour. As Prime Minister she must set an example; she can't be late for the online video-debate. 'If I'm not up to it, I won't last my three months.' The cool shower helps her think.

Senior citizens are lagging behind under-16s in quality of life... Okay, they have the basic things they need: state-of-the-art medical centres in every neighbourhood, adventure playgrounds, two free holidays abroad a year... but there's a serious technology gap. Tony, aged 105 from Cornwall, had emailed her – 'I need a mobicart to get around' – but how many others lack this latest gadget?

The Lower House – average age 13 – understands what it means if nobody listens. Years before Fatima arrived as an unaccompanied asylum seeker in the Federal Republic of SNIWE (Scotland Northern Ireland Wales England), children in England campaigned – even went on school strike – to get their Independent Children's Commissioner championing their rights. (The commissioner later became President.) And Fatima knows about poverty. Only last year, in 2019, was the old people's government pledge to lift all children in SNIWE out of poverty achieved. Much remains to be done on the continent she left behind.

And then there's the elders. The reform of the Upper House – elected by all over-16s – clearly had not brought results.

Her hair still wet, Fatima connects the video-phone.

'Hurry up with your breakfast. Remember today we're talking about tech access for over-16s...' In the Midlands, Rhiordan, her Finance Minister, tired after chatting online with his international friends until midnight, is in no mood to think. Working out economic solutions is fun – but not now.

'Old people have to take things into their own hands. Just as children stopped the AIDS epidemic by occupying the big pharmaceutical companies until they gave the medicines away for free, over-16s need to get into the boardrooms of new tech firms, right? They have to force them to listen to their views.' Not very radical, he knows...

Online, the heated parliamentary debate is short. After all, family-friendly arrangements help members combine work with school or integrated nursery school/PlayStation.

'We have to get the over-16s to learn how to play. They really missed out on traditional games and sports.'

exams, wars and school uniforms were banned long ago

'We've tackled obesity among ourselves, but what about the oldies?'

Fatima reminds them the topic is elder tech-poverty. They vote to invite an over-16s delegation to address the fully accessible House.

Health Minister Orla, 7, as usual gets a bit carried

'We've tackled obesity, but what about the oldies?'

away: 'Let's make it a fun day for everyone: balloons, healthy munching competitions, computer games...'

Fatima packs up her video-mobile and electronic notebook and whizzes down the road on her skateboard. 'Cool. Another day's work done.' Almost. Today, they're doing physics – not her strong point. But at least there are no more exams: they, alongside wars and school uniforms, were banned long ago for being too stressful...

The Future Is Brown (A957837)

by Vaeltaja (U216672) ✪✪✪✪

The first 20 years of the twenty-first century have seen some rather predictable moves in politics. But the consequences were rather more unpredictable! Gordon Brown's economically successful rule as the iron-fisted chancellor was followed by a sharp swing to the left when he took over the Prime Minister's office in 2005.

Perhaps his most remarkable act was to open the floodgates to immigration as Britain accepted workers from all parts of Europe. Despite the initial wave of hostility and resentment from people of every political persuasion, it soon became clear that his was a far-sighted approach.

Within five years of his taking over the leadership of the country, and despite raising taxes openly as well as stealthily, Gordon Brown won his second term as Prime Minister with an increased majority.

Looking back, it was clear to see why. Relaxing immigration rules created a massive injection of younger people with manual skills into a now booming economy. Plumbers, electricians and anyone involved with construction totally changed the way the economy worked.

Suddenly houses, which had long been regarded as derelict and beyond repair, were being renovated. Housing stock rose for the first time in three decades, especially affordable housing. Perhaps even more importantly, the old commitment to getting 50 per cent of school leavers into university was quietly dropped.

The new elite were the skilled crafts people who restored the fabric of society. Able to earn a good living, they also demonstrated that you could plumb in Serbo-Croat or Hungarian – and the lower bills pleased everyone in middle England.

Premier Brown has done a remarkable thing: taken New Labour and turned it back from the Blairite policies towards a form of social inclusion that is based on

the lower bills pleased everyone in middle England

getting the job done – on time, within budget and when you wanted it done. No wonder his proposals for the Socialist Republic of Britain are going down well. Even Charles is willing to vote for that. After all, Highgrove now has some of the best vines in the country, courtesy of Bulgarian winemaking talent!

My New Game (A863354)

by Jennifer Haslam-James (U202280) ✪✪✪

Today I bought a new game for my computer. This one is really good because it forces you to take breaks from it. It won't run for longer than three hours at a stretch without breaking for an hour. You don't lose anything. You just, kind of, go missing to the others for a while. It reactivates when an hour is up, and you put the mask and suit back on, hit the big blue world that will be waiting in front of you, and you jack back in.

Lately there have been a few deaths from people getting so immersed in the game they don't sleep, eat, drink, anything, for days. Only play. That's why they have brought in these time breaks, I think.

I can believe that. I once spent six hours in a game without a break. Eventually it was needing the bathroom that caught me out. That was probably a good thing because it was only when I took the suit off I became aware of how thirsty I was.

So anyway, my new game... In it I'm a secret agent. You get the option of which sex you want to be, and how you want to look. I've chosen to be a girl,

needing the bathroom caught me out

because I am one anyway and I quite like some of the weapons and actions I get with it.

This is one of the reasons I love computer games. In real life, I'm just a plain ordinary girl who wears glasses and has a slight limp from a damaged spine, but in the game I'm gorgeous. I've got long auburn hair tied in a thick ponytail that hangs down to my (tiny) waist and a very cool outfit.

I'm wearing the gaming mask and suit, and now I'm nearly active in the game. I can see options floating and moving up and down slowly in front of me in the form of little coloured worlds that I need to prod in order to choose. I'm ready now. I'm ready to jack into the net and join this new game's world. It's all going on out there in the minds of hundreds and hundreds of other jacked-in people.

I can tell that this is going to be a really good one, and I'm not going to want to leave.

I've also managed to override the three-hour time-out function.

After the boycott of the 2016 Olympic games in Baghdad and the drug-riddled 2012 New York games, the IOC, under President Anne Windsor, strove to ensure there were no scandals this time around, although the relaxing of the rules concerning performance-enhancing drugs marred the event for many.

China topped the medal table again, followed by the USA. The Commonwealth of British States were third, with 49 gold (including the first ever gold medal for ballroom dancing), 72 silver and 102 bronze. Scotland took gold in both carpet bowls (another new event) and one of the shooting events.

At the closing ceremony, London Mayor Steve McFadden handed the Olympic torch to Mayoress Minogue of Melbourne, host of the 2024 games, before fireworks, supplied by Branson Pyrotechnics and costing 80m euros, were set off.

marcos97 (U217471)

Okay, so taking retirement at thirty-five sounds great, and the thought of spending the remaining 70, 80, even 90 years of your life in the VRG (Virtual Reality Game-room) is truly awesome. But getting there is sheer hell, and reversing your option is very costly! Working continuous shifts of 120 hours is more efficient than bursts of eight hours per day. We all have the same mixed feelings about the ultimate decision we made at 15, but I ask you, why should teenagers have to make such big decisions anyway?

However, the pills do the job and keep my world sane and happy. The small amount of money needed to run the VRG and buy food will be easily provided for by my pension, even if I live to 150! The 20 years of hard work I do now will give me 100 years of living in other worlds, playing the latest role games, courtesy of the VRG. It's funny how such a small room can give you so much freedom!

Eddie Smith (U201412)

I haven't made it past level one on 'Mogadishu: Game Park Hell' since I bought it yesterday. Not wanting to blow my own trumpet, but most games don't last beyond 24 hours before I've won. This is different. This is the monster of the games world. If you get to level five you're fighting for real. No larkin' about in virtuality, you have an actual army at your disposal.

JimmyB (U207549)

Superbike 2020 (A948404)
by Dale Sergent (U216081) ✪✪✪

It was not what you'd describe as the tidiest garage, the usual dumping place for out-of-sight, out-of-mind items from the house. I step over and tread between paint pots and, um, stuff that I'm sure will come in handy some day, towards the bike. It's a gleaming metallic blue P1500 XRS: fast, but not an out and out 'speed freaker'. I step over the bike and sit on the seat under the chrome crash bars that run from the back, over me, before splitting to run down either side at the front leaving the front screen clear.

I put the credit card key into the slot and punch in the five-digit security code into the small keyboard set in the top of the dummy tank. The dashboard immediately illuminates and goes through its brief checking procedure. 'Rear tyre will need changing within the next 200 miles, Dale,' the soft female voice tells me. Yeah, yeah, I know. I flip up the side stand, press the starter button with my right thumb and it fires up the five cylinders first time, as always. You think they could have pro-

it fires up the five cylinders first time, as always

grammed it to randomly fire up after the second or third attempt like the cold mornings of yesteryear for a change.

A green light flashes and then remains on,

indicating the engine has reached operational temperature. I pull on the front brake lever and squeeze the left hand that engages the fully automatic gearbox. 'Open,' I command the garage doors and wait for them to silently roll up. I blip the throttle, release the front brake and ease out of the garage, noting next door's dog has crapped in the middle of the driveway again. I hit one of its efforts the other day coming home and nearly slid into the garage.

I select sports mode, blip the engine once more and, with a silly grin on my face, ride out onto the road. 'Hey-ho, hey-ho, its off t…' The dwarves' song is cut short as my head jerks back and I whack open the throttle. While the traction control fights the computerised suspension that's trying to keep both tyres on the road, my grin gets bigger and bigger…

Look Out for Flying Cars! (A949971)

by future facing (U217254) ✪✪✪✪

Flying cars are a familiar sci-fi fantasy that hasn't as yet come tantalisingly close to reality. Given the rising levels of congestion on our roads, it seems inevitable that traffic will eventually take to the skies – but when?

Hoping to meet the challenge are several companies with prototypes that could be mass-produced in a matter of years rather than decades. The most probable in the line-up is the M400 SkyCar from Moller International. With an appearance that has been likened to the Batmobile, you can see the similarity. It has a retro-50s look with its bright red bodywork and four conspicuous propellers. But under the exterior is the car's impressive ability to take off and land vertically using powered lifts, like a Harrier Jump Jet. Four passengers can be transported up to a height of 50 feet and a staggering 390 mph – that's three times faster than any light helicopter.

> the M400 SkyCar with an appearance likened to the Batmobile

With its ability to cover vast distances at great speed, long-distance commuting could become more popular. Other suggested uses include police and fire services – where a speedy response is of utmost importance – express delivery, news reporting and charter flights. Advertised as being far more versatile than a car, or even a helicopter, the price of being free as a bird is expected to be around $500,000 (£305,698), eventually dropping to $60,000 (£36,683).

Another contender in personal flying machines is the SoloTrek XFM (Exo-Skeletor Flying Machine). Simply strap the

machine to your back, and take off and land virtually any-where you want. Tests show that up to 150 miles can be covered, with a speed of up to 80 mph. The manufacturers are primarily aiming the SoloTrek at the military market. With mass production, it could be later aimed at the commercial sector, at a price similar to a 'very high-end sports car'.

These prototypes show that the mechanics are developed to a stage where working models are almost ready to go into mass production. But before you have flights of fancy there's one point that will bring you back down to earth. The regula-tions governing their safety and use in urban areas, like many other new forms of transport, will likely halt the process.

So my advice to those who are worrying about 2020: buy a forecourt, breed some horses and get ready for the demand.

Matthew Zurowski
(11213511)

WALKING BACK TO HAPPINESS (A963830)
BY DIZZYLIZZY (U217401) ✪✪✪✪

I walked to work today. Not that this is in any way an event. I walk to work every day and have done so for nearly 30 years. I sold my last car in 1993 and I have been walking most places ever since. It has taken a long time for others to join me, but as the South East has become ever more densely populated, the need to drive anywhere has been greatly reduced.

The 'concrete jungle' predicted 20 years ago is proving to be a pleasant place to live. Shops, parks, schools and medical facilities are within two miles of most southerners now. There are still some rural areas where motor transport remains a necessity. But here in the South East, anyone living within a 100-mile radius of London is adequately served by the rail and bus networks that

By the year 2010 the daily round of the British commuters had stopped rolling. Overweight, frustrated and enraged, they sat in a crawling jam of over-regulated, expensive and barely mobile cars. Ten years later, a healthy, tanned, playful and optimistic population enjoyed an improved environment, physical and mental balance and the sheer joy of living.

What had worked this miracle? Quite simply, the bicycle. Only the bicycle could, at the same time, pump new life into clogged veins, massively ease congestion on the roads, cut pollution and — using nature's anti-depressant, endorphins — put the pep back into life.

Mark Powell (U214192)

were so greatly improved under the Transport South East legislation of 2010.

More people travel on the waterways too nowadays. Wetter winters and rising sea levels bring the coast ever closer, and I know quite a few people who travel to work by boat. My local council even has plans to introduce a boat bus service!

Plenty of stubborn car-lovers do still drive, but most of them have small electric cars to cover distances of less than 20 miles, and car sharing is becoming more common. There are huge fines for people caught driving petrol-driven vehicles carrying less than three people.

RISING SEA LEVELS BRING THE COAST EVER CLOSER

The pavements are much busier since so many of my fellow workers have discovered walking. The population is becoming fitter and healthier. Some of the larger employers in my hometown offer an increased salary to staff who walk or cycle to work, although I'm not sure how anyone can prove whether they drove in or not. Perhaps we pedestrians look as good as we feel?

When turnout at the general election had reached a new low of 25 per cent, far more votes were expected to be cast in the new series of *Celebrity Big Brother*. All the same, the viewing figures were not expected to rival those for Channel 5's revolutionary reality TV series, *Who Wants to Run a Train Operating Company?*. Jamie Oliver, who won the franchise previously operated by Connex South Eastern, was expected to run all the franchises in Britain after his company, Pukka Rail, introduced novelties such as trains being on time, having enough seats and offering free tickets if the trains were late. Critics accused him of stealing his ideas from state-owned rail companies on the continent.

Aristide (U217770)

Ultra Modern Art (A940222)

by Frankie Roberto (U125489)

At last, here in 2020, we are beginning to see the first new, radical art movement for decades. Ultra-modernism, initiated by a small band of artists living in trendy Grimsby, has sparked a new wave of artistic energy.

The art-establishment, with their roots embedded firmly in traditional modern conceptual art, have refused to accept this new trend as even being art. However, this is widely seen as a cynical move, down to the fact that ultra-modernism has no physical product that can be sold.

For the uninitiated, the basic premise of ultra-modern art is to step away from the idea of art being a creative process. Bored with abstract all-blue paintings and symbolic sculptures, art was refined as 'being' rather than 'creating'. In ultra-modernism, it is the 'self' that is the art - the artist positions

Ultra-modernism has sparked a new wave of artistic energy

their own person, their own lifestyle, as the art.

Critics accuse ultra-modernists as simply being lazy, but artists hit back by saying that it actually takes a lot of effort being them.

Philosophers have really taken to the movement, proclaiming it as the 'true' meaning of art. With 'creative' art you can only put so much meaning into your work. With 'being' art, however, every intellectual thought and action by the artist becomes the art.

Some of the more enthusiastic followers

critics accuse ultra-modernists of being lazy

of the movement have started kidnapping and even killing artists in an attempt at ownership. Many artists have become scared for their lives, and there are fears that the movement might be banned by the government.

Drawings done by human hand are considered the old way. And most artists who draw pictures by hand are older than 60. They are trying to keep hand drawing from dying out.

Kuniko (U221787)

Art events had reached such heights of popularity that queues for the Royal Academy were longer than those for Wimbledon. One couldn't get a look-in without becoming a 'friend'. And then the final realisation dawned: art had attempted to encompass too much. It had lost all focus and it began to implode.

In a desperate bid to reverse the situation, the BBC recruited Cilla Black as its new face for the Arts. More credible institutions attempted to reclaim the aesthetic and intellectual high ground.

AK (U215455)

Red Nose Day 2020 (A979347)

by Surveillance (U218161) ✪✪✪✪

Comic Relief comedians are preparing themselves for their biggest event of the year. In just a few days' time Red Nose Day mania will once again sweep across the nation.

This year the award-winning high-tech red nose – Reacta-Nose – is set to be a huge sell-out with sales already at an all-time high. The proceeds of which go directly to good causes both here in the UK and across the world.

The Reacta-Nose is fully interactive when attached to any networking device and its compact design means it is especially suitable when used with cordless ports on all Interwatches, connecting the user directly to the Comic Relief website. The red nose has certainly come a long way from the tomato-style noses of the 1980s and 90s!

the Reacta-nose is fully interactive

Other highlights of the evening included a live edition of 'Robot Wars', where viewers could participate by controlling robots through their digital television sets, and a special reunion sketch of the 'Men Behaving Badly' duo (Martin Clunes and Neil Morrissey) entitled 'Men Behaving Poorly', where they explored retired life on a state pension.

Cartroo (U203463)

The Catholic Superstate (A873056)

by Ashley Stewart-Noble (U276)

The seeds of the future Catholic Superstate have already been sown by the current Pope, John Paul II. His Holiness is a strong advocate of the Opus Dei, the secretive (they prefer the term 'discreet') organisation that holds a unique position within the Catholic Church.

Opus Dei (God's Work) was founded in 1928 by St José Maria Escriva de Balaguer. Opus Dei now counts well over 80,000 members on three continents: Europe, North and South America. Their task is to carry out the evangelical mission of the Catholic Church through prayer, work and a contribution from their salaries. Membership is by invitation. In October 2002 José Maria Escriva de Balaguer, having been pushed through the fast track for canonisation, was made a Roman Catholic saint.

Members of Opus Dei report to the head office over regional leaders. Children of members also attend special centres and are educated to exceptionally high standards. Once they graduate, many members donate their salaries to Opus Dei and receive a stipend in return. It is these graduates that will blossom into dignitaries, financiers and politicians whose primary function in life is to execute God's work.

Opus Dei will take over the running of the majority of the Catholic schools now in existence and will teach their particular brand of strict education and morals for future leaders. It is the Opus Dei who will openly make the Church money on the stock exchange. Why does a church need such wealth? Well, what price can you put on salvation? The money will go towards creating new centres of learning, new churches and establishing new

what price can you put on salvation?

communities in countries where religion has taken a back seat.

But what is frightening is the immense shift in the global balance of power. With the Pope having the ear of presidents, bankers, ambassadors, generals, monarchs and educators the world over, the true world power (both financial and nuclear) lies in the hands of a man whose followers will follow his order, not those of their elected leaders.

The Holy Goal (A966440)

by geoff anderson (U218278) ✪✪✪✪

At a special press conference to answer her critics, the Dean of St Paul's defended her decision to host the World Snooker Championships in the cathedral until 2030.

She reminded everybody that, when the tournament had been held at the Crucible Theatre in Sheffield, the Crucible had presented a first-rate programme of theatrical productions for the remaining 50 weeks. The same would hold true in her cathedral. She told the director of the National Theatre this morning that his company's tenancy of the cathedral would not be affected.

Declaring the Snooker Box Office officially open she handed out complimentary tickets for the National's production of 'Beckett', wryly commenting that the Dean of Canterbury would miss his favourite play because he would be too busy hosting the World Ice Dancing Championships in his specially refrigerated nave.

Once Liverpool Anglican Cathedral had the idea of turfing their nave to become the home ground of 3rd Division Liverpool FC, cathedrals all over England were quick to get in on the act. The doctor's lucrative deal with the WPSBA is merely the latest in a long line of such arrangements.

The Catholic cathedral in Liverpool has proven to be an ideal circuit for motorbike racing (as all the fumes go up the funnel) and Coventry cathedral is a natural home for athletics, since they can host both the Indoor and Outdoor Championships.

It is rumoured that the biggest marriage of convenience yet is currently at a delicate stage of negotiations – nothing less than bringing the American Football Super Bowl to Westminster Abbey. The sums involved would guarantee the Abbey's survival into the next century. But there is a hold-up. Apparently the Dean is objecting to one of the sponsors' stipulations, that he should use their cola in all future baptisms – the problem being that a rival cola firm already sponsors the Abbey's font.

Doubtless a compromise will be reached and this marvellous scheme will go from strength to strength.

Pope Augustine announced his intention to marry during the traditional Easter Urbi et Orbi address from the balcony of his Vatican apartments. It took a moment or two to sink in – his insistence on speaking in his native Yoruba meant that a translator had to relay his words to the largely Italian crowd – and then a great gasp swept through St Peter's Square. In millions of Catholic homes across the world they marvelled at the latest coup de theatre by the charismatic leader who had changed so much in their Church.

Edward Stourton
(U207957)

Implant Mad (A943139)

by Redyam (U214701)

In the year 2020, the world went implant mad. An amazing array of items could be inserted into your body if you so wished. Even more controversial were the obligatory implants, such as the ID chip that was placed below the nail of the right index finger at birth. Information such as name, nationality, blood group and place of birth were placed into the ID chip to start with, and more information could be added later.

The most popular implant by far was the communication chip. Based upon mobile phone

the US army took the idea of implanting to the extreme

technology, a wireless transmitter/receiver could be inserted into the ear and another microphone placed in a false tooth. The user could phone or communicate with anyone in the world, just by using voice commands.

The credit card chip was also popular. Usually placed within the nail of the left index finger it was used to pay for anything at all, from bus rides to holidays abroad. All you had to do was press your finger on a pad, and a scan of the chip and your fingerprint would be made to pay for the goods.

For the richer residents a number of unique implants were available. These included eye implants, which enhanced the eyesight and added ultra-violet and infrared vision. The ear implants enhanced hearing to such a degree that a user could hear an ant walking up a leaf from ten metres away. A tooth coating was also available, which protected the teeth from tooth decay for at least 50 years.

The US army took the idea of implanting to the extreme. One of the options available was to totally replace the bone structure of a person with a new unbreakable carbon-steel hybrid. The army also gave each soldier a special skin coating made from the same lightweight carbon-steel, which was tough enough to stop a bullet in its tracks, yet light enough to sleep in.

The ultimate implant, the nano-robots that roamed around the body looking for disease to attack, was still years away from being commercially viable, but several successful trials had already been done. The brain was also still a no-go area. Not enough was known about how the brain worked and scientists weren't prepared just yet to experiment.

Evolution (A932177)

by Stuart Smythe (U215193) ✪✪✪✪

I think that in the future we will all have evolved smaller feet for running round corners. Thank you and goodnight.

The Utopia Within (A921908)

by oracleboy (U213636) ✪✪✪✪

I've reached mid-life crisis! Or rather, I've realised that throughout my life I've been moving from one crisis to another. Suddenly I am no longer that zesty 21-year-old with the ability to achieve anything he desired, to feel a positive vitality whilst maintaining a happy disconnection from reality.

No, suddenly I am 35 and life is real and barbed. I did not become a successful musician. I am not a famously published fiction writer. I did not find the one uniting, spiritual way of life. I have not changed the world of politics and ethics. I did not discover that all that we are is tangible and accessibly contained within our genetic material, waiting to be tapped.

No, I have done none of these things yet. If only I could find my disassembled and disillusioned self in this flux of possibilities we call life, then perhaps I could achieve all of the above, at least, in my fictitious universe.

Still, in the year 2020 I will fulfil all of these aspirations, thanks to the radical, life-changing introduction of semi-sentient

nano-technology. After successful experiments in the 2010s on regressive cancer growth and degenerative brain disorders, the medical application of nano-technology will become accepted into western society.

The technology, however, remains open only to the rich and powerful few until the prodigal son of a famous technology billionaire invents the world's first cybernetic brain implant. He will successfully combine this technology with intelligent nano-technology

and release it en masse and free-of-charge to the entire world. Soon people will link directly to the ever-evolving world wide web from the implants in their minds, where anything and everything becomes possible in a cybernetic, virtual universe. It will trigger the greatest leap in human evolution

medical application of nanotechnology will become accepted

and mark the point when humans and machines truly become one altruistic entity.

language

Whither the Withering Apostrophe? (A921827)

by JMM (U213652) ✪✪✪✪

To have 20/20 vision is, of course, a splendid thing. And so, goes the popular adage, is hindsight in similar degree. Reading the articles so far submitted to the editor, one could be confident that the next decade or so will see the demise of the English apostrophe. The following decade will probably see the disappearance of all those who once knew what it was for, and its demise will be total. It will vanish into antiquity along with the semi-colon and words like 'erstwhile' and 'wherefore'.

The apostrophe has led an unhappy life from its first recorded use in the late sixteenth century to signify an omission of one or more

the apostrophe has led an unhappy life

letters in a word, or in the elision on combining two words. It is, by its very nature, a confession of omission, an admission of defeat. So perhaps it is fitting that it, too, is inexorably wending its way to oblivion.

Even the revered OUP advocates dropping the apostrophe from 'The Kings Road' and 'The Rovers Return', leaving us uncertain as to the number of monarchs and wandering home comers involved.

As the apostrophe falls from the common psyche as a tool for indicating omission and, particularly, possession, so it finds new and, to me, entirely inexplicable uses. I suspect that most of my peers, insofar as they can remember back that far, would certainly write '1980's' instead of what I now consider to be the '1980s'. What is the logic for using an apostrophe in this circumstance? I, a man in my 40s [sic], cannot imagine.

We could not possibly 'mind our ps and qs'. Now we might use Ps and Qs, but this somehow imbues the letters with a significance which is over and above their humble purpose (whatever that may be), and cannot be condoned.

So, after some reflection, I may perhaps conclude that the apostrophe is not doomed to extinction, but rather to a re-emergence, phoenix-like from its ashes, preening its new plumage to serve as an inexplicable but indispensable accoutrement in the armoury of the English language.

Telecommuting (CA870671)

by broelan (TU155058) ✪✪✪✪

Air pollution reached mind-boggling proportions in many metropolitan areas in the latter part of the twentieth century. As a result, the leaders of the twenty-first century have seen fit to mandate changes that will stop, and even reverse, the severity of the poisons in our air.

Most noted among these changes is mandatory telecommuting. Most businesses are now required to base a percentage of their office workforce at home. This percentage can vary depending on criteria met, but generally 25 to 60 per cent are home-based employees.

individuals involved reported stronger family units, with less stress and illness

The results of these measures have been entirely favourable. Benefits to businesses include less time lost due to illness, higher productivity and lower operational costs. Home-based employees benefit by being able to spend more time with their families and less time in their autos, and they're saving money on childcare, healthcare and insurance. Individuals involved in a telecommuting environment have reported stronger family units, with less stress and illness.

Diary of a TV Scheduler (A929586)

by Matt Cruse (U214300) ✪✪✪

This morning I logged onto the dole again and made three mugs of tea before the familiar face of the woman finally appeared. She sighed when she recognised me, and proceeded to credit my weekly allowance without hesitation, having seemingly already made up her mind that I had not found work since our last meeting. I pointed out to her, in all politeness, that I felt discriminated against by her automatic conclusion that I was apparently unemployable, to which she said something along the lines of 'you lot always are'. When I questioned her about what 'my lot' actually meant, she simply referred to 'those who think they know what everyone else wants to watch and when they want to watch it'.

This, of course, is what I get all the time nowadays. However much I say (as I always do in situations like this) that it was virtually unheard of for one of my peers to be voted in as Prime Minister, the public assume that politics is the 'new home' of the now-defunct TV scheduler. It's just a passing fad. Some of us are destined to rise again in our chosen field to be better, faster and stronger than ever before.

The woman stared at me down her monitor screen and started to jab her light-pen at me as she spoke. She explained that she had a little grey box at home with a little red button on it, and that button

I was apparently unemployable... 'you lot always are', she said

allowed her to watch whatever she wanted, whenever she wanted, however she wanted it, and even to get whatever it was to pause automatically while she was 'doing it' (which wasn't a regular occurrence for her these days but she was trying to make a point). And, if she was feeling really adventurous, she could watch the whole thing again straight afterwards without having to wait for someone like me to decide that it was time for her to see it again two years later at some god-forsaken unsociable hour when she'd be asleep anyway.

I blurted out, not so politely this time, that all this watch-it-when-you-want-it rubbish was just a big gimmick and the world still needed TV schedulers with their intricately devised entertainment menus.

The woman slid the light-pen behind her ear, folded her arms and said that she'd had two entire scheduling teams and an audience researcher in that morning, with not a single trace of any little red button manufacturers, and that I should 'do the maths'. Leaning back in my chair, I announced that our time would come and tried to manufacture a dramatic logout, but my computer created a fatal exception error and left me hanging in the room allowing the woman to leave first, shaking her head as she went.

Tomorrow, I'm due to log in to the Job Centre again. Can't wait.

We are proud to launch our new range of dynamic, low-maintenance, compact, call-centre staff.

Key features include:
▼ A simplified 'human' brain consisting of short-term memory and basic verbal skills.
▼ Glass jar, feeding tubes, etc.
▼ Hardwired sockets for all popular makes of telephone and office equipment.
▼ A year's supply of nutrient solution. No more bulky vending machines or sandwich trolleys!
▼ A year's supply of Nescaffaine™ sleep regulator powder supplements. How many of your employees can work a 22-hour day, every day, seven days a week?
▼ A range of voice settings, including 'Trustworthy Northern Bloke', 'Perky 18-Year-Old Girl', and 'Thora Hird'.
▼ Free accessories including a car cigarette lighter adapter and a range of attractive jar lids.

Jon Rowett (U219419)

In 2020 we will see a large displacement of office-bound staff to the home or to 'service farms', probably located away from major cities, like out of town shopping centres. As information becomes more freely available over the Internet, so we will recognise that information, and the people who own it / know how to manage it, will be the core assets of a business.

Mark Aldridge (U214788)

Brunette on the Greenway (A935769)
by Researcher 214654 ✪✪✪✪

5:55 p.m. Oh no, I better get to the car before I lose my slot and the attractive brunette. Since Prescott's 'Greenways' got the go-ahead, everybody's timekeeping has sure improved, I know that much.

But, sadly, not their organisation. Every morning I promise to sort out my TerraBox: download the files I need, give it a good clean out. But with enough capacity to save everything I'll ever do on the size of a couple of cigarette boxes, why bother? (Ah, cigarettes, do you remember them?)

The new Greenway system works well though – exactly 47 minutes door-to-door, every day. You just jump in your car and hit the button. That's it – whisked home at the most fuel-efficient speed, exactly 2.2 car-lengths from the car in front, driven by the attractive brunette. Well, I say 'driven' - of course, you just sit there and stare out the window, watch the news or plug in your TerraBox and get some more work done.

She must live near me – the brunette, I mean. Our cars follow virtually identical routes, which means the Greenway Traffic Guidance System must have plotted this as her most efficient time and route to travel, just like me. Don't even think about requesting an alternative travelling slot. Requests fall on deaf ears. (This, of course, assumes there is someone at the central control feigning deafness.) A couple of years ago I got stuck in a meeting with a very important client and missed my slot. Six hours later I got reassigned a new slot and it cost me 45 Green Credits, which I think is

'Hi, my name's Susan. I'm in the car in front... if you'd like to share a lift'

about £60 after tax. Bastards.

My company say they can make the cars even more efficient; but they would – they're a petrol company. All credit to them, they managed to abolish trains back in 2016 in favour of CarTrack. Essentially, everyone's car acts as an individual carriage and you get Green Credits for giving other people a lift around the country. Quite a good idea, unless you get a sweaty salesman with a formidable line in boring stories. Still, it paid for my trip to Edinburgh.

Hey, a message. 'Hi, my name's Susan. I'm in the car in front. If you'd like to share a lift sometime, it would save us both Green Credits.'

Prescott, I love you – and there aren't too many people who have said that!

"SON, YOU'RE OLD ENOUGH NOW TO KNOW WHERE YOU CAME FROM ....YOUR FATHER AND I BOUGHT YOU ON E-BAY."

DIY Relationships (A956450)

by SW (U217181) ✪✪✪✪

It's been three years since I've had what I would call a steady relationship. Not an unremarkable story – it just sort of fizzled out once we'd finished renovating the house. It was as if all that sanding and plastering had taken all the life out of us. When we'd finished this grand renovation we had nothing to say to each other because there was nothing left to sand. We could navigate around B&Q better than we could navigate around each other.

Anyway, he ran off with a girl from a website who was building an extension to her house. There was a craze where single women would advertise their DIY needs on a website in return for a date. You could get some shelves put up and some company all at the same time. That's where he met her.

I tried it once, but this guy was not only lying about his age, but also about his NVQ in plumbing. It was a disaster. He was nice enough; we met in a wine bar on the Fulham Road. He collected tools. I think he had some sort of fetish, carrying this mail-order catalogue around with him called Screw-it. Anyway, it didn't last long and the plumbing never got done.

I had a quick look on 'Love in a Box' on cable the other day. John from Harrow looked quite cute, but his story was very dull and he could have done with some make-up. He was keen on DIY and had been on the property ladder since 2005, so a good catch. I added John to my video favourites and tagged him as a possible.

Personal Silence (A964307)

by Geggs Sakkosekken (U201647) ✪✪✪✪

Ever find your train of thought interrupted by journalists? Ever wish the person that keeps phoning you would just go away and stop annoying you? Do you feel that life would be much nicer if you didn't hear your partner moaning? Then Personal Silence is for you!

Our scientists, hidden in a secret Alpine lab, began work back in 2017, analysing the basic constituents of silence. They took recordings from deep valleys and mountain peaks all across the range and, utilising advanced aural-mixing methods, compared the various recordings in order to obtain a base-line silence.

Armed with that model we were able to obtain silences from all around the world: the frozen wastes of the Antarctic, the lush woods of Peru, the rather dull valleys of Wales and the placid Sea of Tranquillity. We blended all of these together to make a perfect, ultimate silence for your use.

Personal Silence comes in two forms, both available at a very reasonable price.

Firstly, there's the Silence Field Generator. Simply attach the SFG to your clothing and you will be enveloped in a Silence Field extending a mere nano-metre from the surface of your body. No sounds will penetrate this field, so that you can pass your whole day in blissful silence.

The second, far more discreet, option is the Silence Chip. Following a simple operation this chip will reside inside your head, connected to your neural pathways and the auditory tract. If you want silence at any time, day or night, just think it, and silence will fill your ears, blocking out all sounds!

Buy Personal Silence today. SFG available from 29.99 euros. SC from 59.99 plus additional costs.*

*Additional costs depend on the cost of operations at your nearest robotics hospital.

would life be much nicer if you didn't hear your partner moaning?

Re-inventing Light, Sleep and Society (A935705)

by râc·òó·n (U215115)

In 2020, the world shall celebrate the birth of the revolutionary light bulb that produces what will be referred to as the 'black light'. Very much similar to the latest 'noise cancelling' technology, the new light bulb takes advantage of the interference pattern of visible light. It emits similar light rays, causing destructive interference that would eventually 'cancel out' all the visible light within a certain radius, thus creating the illusion of pitch black darkness.

This new invention will enable people to sleep during the day. People that will benefit include those who work night-shift jobs, those who travel internationally and perhaps those who've done just a little bit too much partying the previous night.

With the proliferation of such technology in cities, more and more people will

> a revolutionary lightbulb 'cancels out' all the visible light

be able to work and play at night. A new class of night-workers will emerge, and the advantages will be countless.

For instance, these night-workers will require goods and services just like the rest of us morning-workers. With the same numbers of consumers demanding services almost 24/7, businesses will keep their doors open. As a result more jobs will be created to serve the customers, and naturally we shall see a decline in unemployment. A working day will consist of the day's full 24 hours. Therefore, more work will get done in the same amount of time and society will advance faster than ever before. We might see our childhood fantasies turn into reality in our lifetime.

If working is of no interest to you, how about longer parties during weekends? Since the sun can no longer drag you out of your bed the next morning, you won't be restless and cranky for the rest of your weekend!

To be hilarious is the idea, and to stretch your imagination is the purpose. But there could be dearth of possibilities when the imagination is not far fetched.

Dr Hamid Ishaq (U210344)

24/7 (A949791)

by Dylan (U216871) ✪✪✪✪✪

Global Voice – The World's Paper
Thursday, 22 January 2020

New York, the city that never sleeps, is literally to become just that.

24/7, a Chinese pharmaceutical company, today released details of plans to put New Yorkers on a two-year drug trial. With the people's consent, next month 24/7 will begin issuing a new wonder drug called Orexin.

First developed to restore the sleep patterns of narcoleptics in 2003, Orexin manifested an interesting side effect in people without the condition. It suppressed the need for sleep.

Early experiments resulted in people forming an addiction to non-stop lifestyles and consequently burning out. Efforts to fine-tune the drug failed and left burning holes in pharmaceutical company pockets.

Aptly staged in Times Square, 24/7 Chairman Matt Irving addressed New York: 'This is the beginning of a perpetual new dawn, and one that will change the face of humanity forever.'

Thinking the Unthinkable (A958656)

by Chris Morris (U215795)

To guess where our society is going we need to know where it came from. The modern world that we, particularly in the English-speaking community, so take for granted is essentially a product of the seventeenth century's scientific revolution and the subsequent Enlightenment period. This was, in effect, the search for some absolute truth not derived from Aristotle or the Bible, upon which could be constructed a society where all citizens would be treated

the rigid social structure of the medieval world was broken down

equally. It was a success to the extent that, having emptied the term 'God' of its meaning, the rigid social structure of the medieval world (built around the idea that God made the world perfectly fixed and unchangeable) was broken

down and many great statements of democratic ideals, such as the US Constitution, were written.

But, as Alisdair McIntyre has argued, the project eventually failed to discover any single, over-riding principle that would provide a rational structure for a truly democratic society. The three most notable attempts to implement such a principle have all failed: fascism, because it is too rigid and parochial to outlive the person who embodies it; communism, because Marx couldn't bear to admit that Hegel might be right; and, of course, capitalism.

Has capitalism failed? The path of free-market individualism it followed has given capitalism the flexibility to adapt to many different cultures. Yet, individualism is a dead-end. Humans can only be social animals and, as that well-known anarchist Margaret H. Thatcher informed us, for the true free-marketer 'there is no such thing as society'. Hence, the obsession in Postmodernism for reconnecting individuals with some sort of social structure. But this can't be the old society of masses of the modern world; it has to be a menu of sub-cultures and interest groups from which we can choose at random and transiently.

What does this mean for our future? Capitalism seems to be reaching the limit of its adaptability. The old certainty of the modern world, where most people could expect free education and healthcare, long-term, stable employment and a pension is disappearing rapidly. It could be that, when George Bush (Sr) declared that the 'free world' had won the Cold War he was making one of his worst verbal gaffes. Communism, like capitalism, is another facet of the industrial age and its demise is more likely to be just another event in the downfall of that age. The transition from pre-modern to modern society was accompanied by the Hundred Years War. Perhaps George Bush (Jr) is now beginning a second Hundred Years War, as blissfully ignorant of history as his father.

Since the certainty presented by the social sciences and the corresponding concept of 'progress' central to the ideology of the modern world are increasingly seen to be an illusion, large numbers of people are desperately trying to return to the pre-modern certainty of religion. However, as noted earlier, this is an empty term. Consequently people can, in a very post-modern fashion, fill it with any content they choose – hence the growing number of fundamentalisms, sects and cults. This very choice will be the downfall of religion, as it will lead to increasing dissatisfaction and conflict – not perhaps within the next seventeen years, but soon enough.

It was confirmed by the United Nations today that DeXMac International, the world-wide management and engineering consultancy group, has been successful in its application to be officially recognised as a country.

Astrotomato

(U207003)

Britain and the European Union 2020 (A918641)

by Patong (U211997) ✪✪✪✪

The decisive factor in Britain's future will no doubt be the development of the European Union. The EU's current economic situation, and that of their most influential member states (i.e. France, Germany), is quite modest. By 2020 at least ten countries, possibly thirteen or more, will have joined the EU, which will probably be renamed the 'United States of Europe'.

Experts predict that the enlargement will bring peace, prosperity and a better quality of life, since most of the new member states are, relatively speaking, poor and have a huge potential for economic growth. In reality, however, only the new member states will benefit economically, at the cost of the others. There will be de-polarisation: the poor countries will be less poor and the rich countries less rich.

The main reason for this pessimistic view is that most of those new countries have been culturally neglected and psychologically drained by communist regimes for decades, and any prediction that is entirely concluded from economical growth figures cannot tell the whole story. In a social context, it would be difficult for any society to properly integrate such a rapid historical change. An example is Russia, where the communist oppressors were swiftly replaced by the capitalist mafia.

Overcrowding will also become worse on our island, as there is only a limited amount of space but more people will want to immigrate. Some obvious problems are that Britain's labour market will be swamped by cheap and low-quality man-power. Organised crime will be able to operate even more easily, not only penetrating every aspect of business but also bringing violent crime and prostitution. The latter is already flourishing in the eastern European countries thanks to the demand from western European citizens. A more rigorous monitoring of civil and human rights will make it very difficult to fight organized

the USE will become the world's second superpower

crime and the ultimate point of the other end of the spectrum is a city in chaos similar to Chicago in 1930.

The USE will become the world's second super power and will develop a kind of economic cold-war with the USA, which will not want to give up its superior global position, especially when it comes to issues such as access to the economies of developing countries. And alongside all these will be the possibility of devastating terror attacks, religious uprising, natural disasters and other unpredictable factors which could contribute to upsetting an unstable Britain even more.

Socio-economic Democracy (A935435)

by RobGeorge (U215657) ✪✪✪✪

Profound and unexpected, the planetary Politicosocioeconomic Transformation was well underway by 2020. Enthusiastic discussions and actual implementation of various forms of Socioeconomic Democracy were taking place globally. Looking backward to 2003, it happened so fast!

Across Clinton's 'Bridge to the Twenty-First Century', the folks living back at that time encountered the Gates of Hell. You will recall that outrages visited them daily, assaulting their senses and sensibilities. Mega-scandals were emanating from the arenas of politics, business, finance, economics, government, commerce, geopolitical/military policy-making and taxation to mention just a few. Remember the attempted wealth redistribution from the hard-working poor and what was left of the middle class to the already extremely wealthy? Mankind appeared as bereft of new ideas as any Marxist and simply whimpered, denied and suffered obediently.

Yet the potential for positive change, which is always optimistically growing, blossomed to beautiful fruition about twenty years back. As it was defined from the beginning, Socioeconomic Democracy was and remains a model socioeconomic system wherein there exists both some form of universally guaranteed personal income and some form of maximum allowable personal wealth limit, with both the lower bound on personal material poverty and the upper bound on personal material wealth, set and adjusted democratically by all participants of society.

Thinkers such as Thales, Plato and Aristotle, as well as Tom Paine and Tom Jefferson, on down through the many globally distributed progressive thinkers of the nineteenth and twentieth centuries, had all pleaded for similar solutions. The work of the Nobel prize-winning economists Kenneth Arrow and Amartya Sen established the mathematically correct procedure by which society could democratically set the two fundamental socioeconomic bounds: namely, the median values of the voters' preferences.

Research had justified the basic tenets and predictions of Socioeconomic Democracy from anthropological, philosophical, psychological, religious and human rights perspectives. That Socio-economic Democracy was similar to Zakat, one of the five pillars of Islam, allowed what was then called the 'clash of civilizations' to be theoretically resolved peacefully.

What really made the difference was the new, societally synergetic economic incentives created by the new democratic socioeconomic arrangements. With these incentives, still acknowledging self-interest but now employing rational analysis, the torrent of troublesome and indeed lethal situations engulfing the globe nearly twenty years ago are now starting to evaporate.

POLITICS-2020 STYLE

The SPHINCTER Monologues-No.1
Well, Ladies and Gentlemen, that was a bugger, wasn't it? Thank God it's all over, that's what I say. I don't need to lie to you anymore. All those wild promises we have all been making- forget it! They were all porky pies. You were right all along, but I told you what you wanted to hear and that's my job even though many of you haven't got one! Ha-ha!! Only joking-see what we can do, but I can't promise anything, not now. No point really if you see what I mean...etc...blah............blah...blah.........

Sponsored by The NEW BREED of OAP Freedom Fighters
(Savage Satirist with a Bus Pass).

BBC Book of the Future Scandal (A923519)

by Mark Pettifer (U213114) ✪✪✪✪

An estimated sum of £20 million was split 9,000 ways as the BBC settled out of court with those whose ideas submitted in the 2003 *Book of the Future* revitalised the ailing corporation.

'Our backs were against the wall,' a leading BBC executive said this morning, 'We just could not compete with the commercial multi-media corporate giants. We had to do something.'

Over the last seventeen years such popular shows as *My Fluffy Ginger Cat Was Really An Alien From Somewhere Else* and *How Long Has Bush Really Been Dead?* that topped the ratings had all come from the BBC project. These two shows alone have netted well in excess of £20 million in their first season and, with off-shoots and merchandising, that figure is likely to rise to £40 million by Christmas.

The Internet, which had invited people to write for the book, was used to commence intellectual property legal actions in 2004, when several contributors saw their ideas on primetime TV with no warning or recognition.

In 1987, the nine-hundredth anniversary of the Domesday Book, the BBC celebrated by creating their own, modern book called the Domesday Project. To ensure that the book was available for posterity, it was recorded onto a set of laserdiscs, readable only by the venerable Acorn microcomputer.

Now while the Domesday Book is still incredibly readable and may be viewed at the Public Record Office in Kew, when researchers returned to the BBC's Domesday Project they found that they could not reclaim the information stored less than two decades previously.

Book of the Future – Look to the past!

Casanova the Short (U118008)

Remembering the Book of the Future – an eighteenth birthday tribute (A978258)

by Keith Bullock (U216682) ✪✪✪✪✪

The *Book of the Future* has long held pride of place in the London Museum of Humankind. Now, as the book comes of age with the approach of 2021, this newspaper is proud to offer a fresh evaluation of its historical importance. The Zoggian Homological Research Institute of New York has frequently acknowledged that nothing was more singularly important to our success here, than our *Book of the Future*.

The courage and resourcefulness of the *Book of the Future* editors in those dark and dangerous times has passed into folklore as one of the most thrilling chapters in our inter-planetary history. Despite daily contact with some of the biggest literary egos of humankind, despite the tremendous risks of exposure via the feedback pages, despite daily 'liquid lunches' and evenings out on the town, feigning human-type enjoyment, somehow they came through, undetected, intact and Zoggianistically unspoiled.

The rest, as they say, is history. Through the *BotF* we came to understand the human mind and all of its future machinations. We understood where man was going. We had captured the cream of his thinking – from badinage on Body and Mind to entreaty on the Environment, from speculation on Spirituality to postulation on Politics and Society – we had it all.

Who can say whether we were cruel or kind to preserve the existence of a selection of those forward-thinking human scribes? (A few can still be seen during opening hours in the Whipsnade Homological Park.) Of course, as futurologists, what big-time losers they were! Perhaps life, on whatever terms, is preferable to extinction – and for this, they have their early talents to thank. As for we Zoggians, we literally owe them the Earth.